FORWARD

The taboos related to sex, sexuality and one's sexual preferences are the most challenging as anyone deviating from the so-called normal person is seen as threat to the societal control which thrives on the subjugation of individual freewill. Picking up the story of Tina, author Sunaina has taken up the challenge of providing a platform to the marginalised and victimised section of society to voice their plight and trauma. The author doesn't present Tina's struggles as a bisexual from a vantage point, she rather makes the reader walk hand in hand with the protagonist through each stage of her struggle, confusion, guilt, heartbreak and victimisation. It's a heart touching story of a woman fighting for her identity and respect in society. Though there is recognition of the rights of LGBT community, yet there is still a long way to go as far as social sensitisation is concerned. These are the stories that need to told to move towards a more tolerant society and The Purple Couch is certainly a step in that direction.

Geetu Vaid
Deputy Editor,
The Tribune, Chandigarh

FORWARD

A bold attempt with the subject by my friend as she paces ahead in her creative journey through writing. The struggles of the protagonist to embrace her individuality and to be her own person is inspiring for anyone who chooses a challenging life path to be able to express who they really are. The narrative of the book is the author's expression of a changing world. When it comes to human emotions and the struggle can be very different for each individual. The book encompasses the sheer beauty of spirit, grit and perseverance that is the strength of the woman protagonist in the novel who fights for her dignity and stands by her life choices. Wishing Sunaina all the very best.

Anuradha Shukla
Editor, News 18

The Purple Couch

A reality that yearns to be accepted…

(Based on a true story)

SUNAINA
SINDHWANI

Title : **The Purple Couch - A reality that yearns to be accepted**

Author : **Sunaina Sindhwani**

Copyright © **Sunaina Sindhwani** 2022

All rights reserved

First published in 2022

First Edition 2022

ISBN : 978-93-93262-25-7

A special thanks to my co author and daughter..**Ruhi Sindhwani** to bring this book out to see the light of the day.

Dedicated To

LGBTQIA+ Community

NAM-MYO-HO-RENGE-KYO

Acknowledgements

Since 2020, when I met her, she had always been on my mind. And one special day, on December 16, 2021, I decided to write about her.

Thank you to my lovely daughter Ruhi (Co Author), my adorable son Gottam and my very loving husband Vinay, who pre-launched the cover of this book, The Purple Couch… based on a true story

It wasn't an easy journey for me, but the Universe kept on sending angels in many forms to help.

My heartfelt gratitude to my parents, my sister Geetu Ralen, my mother in law, who has always supported me in my writing endeavors.

Thank you to my dear friend Sundeep Kottaki who introduced me to the real Tina.

Thank you to Lifestyle Magazine for first talking about the book.

Thank you to Ms Dhanajay Chauhan from Saksham Trust, Chandigarh, for supporting this noble cause and inviting me to speak about LGBTQS on various platforms.

Thank you to my dear friend Anuradha Shukla, (Editor, News 18), Karan Verma, Abhishek from News 24 , Gagan from Punjab News and Khushbu from HolyBolly Baba YouTube channel. They all interviewed me on their platforms and created a big buzz about the book on social media.

Thank you so much to Dr Deepti Verma and her super accelerated group members who always encouraged me by teaching me the "Gratitude Practices" by Rhonda Byrne which made my writing journey very special. I shall remain grateful to them.

Thank you to Mr Madhusheel Arora for always supporting me.

Thank you to all SGI members, Calgary.

Thank you to my publisher Prashant Gupta for his phenomenal support in helping me publish this book through his Holistic Publication House.

A big thank you to my editor.

A special thanks to Mr. Madhusheel Arora for helping me bringing this book to various platforms.

Thank you to my author friends Nilanjana Chatterjee and Aditya Narayan for their all weather support.

Thank you, Thank you, Thank you Universe for this book which I really hope will touch hearts of millions and illuminate their lives too.

Happy Reading

With the exception of Tina, all names and
identifying details have been changed to
protect the privacy of Tina's family.

Contents

Prologue

A CHANCE MEETING   1

THE BIRTHDAY PARTY   4

THE AFTERMATH   9

LOSSES AND A DARK HOLE OF DESPAIR   12

DON'T LOOK BACK…EVER   17

A LOVED ONE LEAVES AND A PREDATOR
ATTACKS   21

A MIND IN CHAOS   26

THE NEED TO TELL LIES   30

DID TINA LIE TO ME..   36

ARROWS FLY THICK AND FAST   39

BETRAYAL   43

BLOWING HOT AND COLD   49

REKINDLED HOPES   53

THE ENEMY STRIKES AGAIN   58

SEEDS OF DISHARMONY   64

MELTDOWN AND MISUNDERSTANDINGS 70

INTO DARKNESS 75

TRYING HARD TO HOLD ON 79

MISTAKING LUST FOR LOVE 85

GETTING OVER HEARTBREAK 92

A WONDERFUL SURPRISE 98

ACTING ON IMPULSE 108

AN IRRESISTIBLE OFFER 111

THE SURPRISE PROPOSAL 114

CONDITIONAL LOVE 119

REAWAKENING 123

FLEEING 131

DIVINE GUIDANCE 139

REACHING OUT 142

TO STAND ALONE IN THE CROWD 148

Epilogue

PROLOGUE

The Purple Couch – Love, loss and redemption: A woman's painful quest for the truth

As much as I tried to, I could not forget her face. Tina had welcomed me with flowers at my friend Sandeep's NGO in Hyderabad, where I had been invited to talk about women's empowerment and talk about my first book, I Breathe Last For You. It was a tribute to a friend who, lost her life due to exploitation at toxic work cultures., and chosen to tragically cut short her journey on earth.

Though tired after the early morning rush to Chandigarh airport for the two-hour flight to Hyderabad, I was cheered up and refreshed by the beautiful smiling faces of the women and girls – resplendent in white and gold bordered Kasavu saris – greeting me at the NGO. .

Discussions around my book had just begun, when I heard a knock on the door. As I looked up, Tina, who had remained outside all this while, walked in. I stood up to shake her hand while Sandeep introduced her as a full-time counsellor in his NGO to women and teenagers dealing with sexual abuse. Something about her was arresting. She was beautiful, but the pain in her eyes could not be missed. Her soft voice, "Welcome, ma'am," touched my heart.

Then, when I learnt that despite being a wife and mother she had been living for the last five years in the NGO's office premises, I realized there was more to Tina's story than what was being revealed..

What was it about Tina that I could not forget? What was hidden in the pain in her heart that reached her eyes? What was her story?

Could I reach out to her and get her to speak about it? Could it help other women in a similar situation?

That was the moment when the seed of another book about a woman's painful journey to seek her own reality was sown…

I picked up the phone to dial Sandeep to see if I could set up a meeting with Tina again.

This book is about her.

Chapter 1
Back again in Hyderabad

I was overcome with uneasiness as the taxi moved out of Hyderabad Airport . This was my second trip from Chandigarh to the Hyderabad within hours. I felt tired, exhausted and full of doubts. Was my intuition correct? Why did I feel the need to connect to Tina, the woman I met during my last visit. Why couldn't I get her out of my mind?

Yes, I had been impulsive. After Sandeep's call the night before, I had not given a second thought to the voices in my head urging me to take it easy and not go on a wild goose chase simply to look for the story that I thought was hidden in Tina's heart. But Sandeep had been encouraging. "She's an interesting person, a star worker at my NGO who goes out of her way to help other women and children. Sadly, she has no time for anything but work."

Sandeep said he had known many women who had chosen to give up the fight. Very few had the courage and a strong will to move on and forget the past. Each person has a story that can be a lesson for others. Come and meet Tina, he said..

And that's why I was back in the city where Tina worked. Sandeep was there to receive me and took me straight to my room without stopping for tea or coffee. Once he had left, I dialed Tina's mobile phone at around 8 pm, asking if she could come over to meet me.

She was there in 15 minutes, dressed casually in a T-shirt and jogging bottoms, alert and curious.

The first question she asked me was a polite "How can I help you?" as she settled down in a chair.

A little awkward now, realizing that I had to set the ground carefully for a conversation about her personal life, which was definitely a sensitive matter, I opened with: "How are you doing? I hope I'm not disturbing you."

I was relieved to know she had been free for the evening and, as a matter of fact, had been planning to call me to discuss my book. "I found it interesting, especially how you managed to convey the emotions of a person in despair. You know how to connect to your readers," Tina said.

"That is why I'm here again", I interrupted her, eager to get over the stress of the initial awkwardness and coming straight to the topic on top of my mind.

"I do not understand," was Tina's question, now with a tinge of anxiety.

I could see she was getting restless, so I got up and offered her a glass of water and put my hand on her shoulders, wanting her to relax.

It was a gentle question: "Is there something you want to share with me? Sometimes I know it helps to unburden one's heart."

As I held my breath in anticipation of her answer, I saw tears in her eyes, which were already saying yes to me and then she started …..

CHAPTER 2
The birthday party

Tina belonged to Dehradun, a beautiful city in the Himalayan foothills, renowned for its elite Indian Military Academy, its premium private schools, lakes, saints, and spiritualism. Living in a joint family with her grandparents, paternal uncle and aunts, and being the only girl child with five male cousins, she was the lucky recipient of an abundance of love and care.

As hers was a conservative family, the idea of Tina playing outdoors was frowned upon by the elders. The company of her brothers, however, was enough for her.

The only cloud on the horizon, was the constant teasing by everyone for her tomboy looks , her close-cropped hair, thin frame and her shorts, trousers and shirts. This was part of a family tradition that all children till the age of five years wear clothes their cousins had outgrown.

Though Tina protested against this at times, her mother Sarika, always overburdened with household duties, had no time to pay heed to her complaints.

Despite her academic accomplishments, Sarika had chosen to stay at home and devote all her time to her family, especially her child. She had no regrets about this. The only thing that bothered her, however, was her in-laws' interference in her daughter's upbringing.

Tina on her part was very close to her grandparents and loved every minute spent with them, especially when her grandmother told her stories.

Then there were other things on the little girl's mind.

She was turning six years old on February 16 and waiting eagerly for her birthday, when her parents had promised to get her a beautiful pink frock and matching shoes. A big party was being organized at home for friends and family members.

The only spoil on her happiness was that her aunt's cousins Raj and Dev, 10 years older than her, had also been invited and she did not like them much. They would tease her by calling her Tom and laughing at her… and she wondered what their reaction would be to see her dressed in all her finery and girly clothes.

When the day arrived, it started wonderfully with much fun and laughter. After balloons were burst, the cake was cut and everyone had feasted on the delicacies, Tina excitedly unwrapped her gifts, exclaiming happily each time she discovered a beautiful doll or a book of fairy tales.

Everything was fine until Tina tore open a gift parcel to find a pair of shorts from Raj and Dev. It had 'Tom' stitched on in bold colours.

Tina felt she had just enough. Bursting into tears, she fled from the living room to her bedroom and closed the door behind and her family members got surprised and anxious.

As Sarika had been watching her daughter Tina, she swiftly got up from the sofa and followed her. Finding her slumped on her bed, she hugged Tina and murmured soothingly. "You're a big girl now and you have got a lovely dress for your birthday, no one will be able to tease you now that you can wear anything you want to."

"When will my hair grow?" Tina asked, looking up, her face streaming with tears. "Very soon," Sarika reassured her, affectionately running her fingers through her daughter's hair.

Both sat there, comforted with each other's presence. By and by, after calming down, Tina decided she wanted some fun, and so left her room to go all around the house looking for her cousins.

All of them were in a room playing video games and welcomed her.

Soon, however, even as she was laughing and indulging in some good-natured banter with them, Dev and Raj walked into the room and asked Tina to leave, saying they wanted to watch videos with the other boys. They were in no mood to listen to her pleas to hang out with them.

Tina was in tears again as the door shut behind her with the laughter of the boys following her. After walking around for a while and realising that her newly opened gifts were no match for her curiosity over what her brothers were doing, she went back to the closed door and pushed.

It wouldn't open and the silence inside almost seemed to clutch at her throat. Why should she be left out when they had fun? Wasn't it her birthday after all?

Unable to stand it a moment longer, Tina climbed the tall cabinet near the door and peeked in through the window above.

The boys were quietly watching a video with their backs to her so she could not read their expressions. The fan whirled silently, cutting through the warm air. It seemed to be a peaceful space.

But then Tina's eyes went to the television screen to see what was playing.

For a moment her mind did not register anything. But when the images, one melding into another, sometimes sharp and hazy, started to make sense, Tina froze in horror.

And as she stood there, looking in, Raj turned his head and his eyes fell upon her.

CHAPTER 3
The Aftermath

Confused and dazed by what she saw, Tina took refuge in her room again, not paying heed to calls from her aunt to come downstairs for dinner.

Worried about the sudden change in her daughter's behaviour again, Sarika went into Tina's room and finding her crouched on the bed, looking distraught, held her tight.

But Tina refused to say anything.

As it was late, Sarika coaxed Tina to have dinner and then took her to her own bedroom, where she snuggled between her parents and slept soundly through the night.

The little girl was quiet and preoccupied the next morning while getting ready for school, where her cousins studied too.

Much to her parents' surprise, she refused to

accompany them that day. Her father, usually a quiet and reserved person, too sensed something was wrong and willingly agreed to drop her when she requested him to do so.

Once at school, Tina made it a point to remain focused on studies and not seek out her cousins during the break or have lunch with them. Her cousins also kept to themselves.

Later, when taking the school bus home, Tina made sure she sat in the last row, far away from where she usually sat with her cousins.

Sid, who was one of Tina's favourite brothers despite being five years older, was upset to see her in such a state. He also understood that last night's events were serious enough to get scolded from the elders in the household as Tina's behavior was giving them clues about what the boys did last night..

Tina looked terrified as Sid got up from his seat to come and sit next to her, but he caught her arm and gently asked her to calm down.

"Look Tina," he started. "I know you are very upset with what you saw the other day. But you have to understand that boys are different. They are usually curious about a lot of things. At one stage when one is growing up, one wants to know a lot about physical relationships between a man and a woman. You should not take it seriously. Forget everything. We are your brothers and we love you very much. You know that."

Tina chose not to respond, but her conflicting emotions brought on another wave of tears. As the bus halted at her stop, she was relieved to see her mother waiting for her and ran into her arms.

Once in her room, Tina kept crying, not stopping till her mother got her water, wiped her tears and persuaded her to tell her what was bothering her.

After a while, when she was composed enough to talk, Tina poured out the truth, watching Sarika's expression change from concern to sadness as she realized how, within minutes, this six-year-old girl's life had changed.

Chapter 4
Losses and a dark hole of despair

In the days that followed Tina's tearful outburst, Sarika kept a watchful eye on her, asking her to forget everything she had witnessed, advising her to "imagine it to be a movie, a hallucination of someone's imagination." Realizing, she had to move on, Tina tried to put the unpleasant episode behind her and slowly made an effort to mend her ties with her cousins, desperately trying to normalize everything.

Her eighth birthday came and went on February 16 without much ado, a beautiful new frock with laces and frills adding to her joy. Her hair had grown long too, making her look very feminine. This time her mother actually listened to her pleas to invite a few selected friends and not Raj and Dev.

This was also a time when the young girl had

started growing up, her features sharpening, adding to her charms. She was more secretive now even as she busied herself with studies and household chores.

At times, however, Tina went back to her dolls, playing with them for hours in what seemed to be her last fling with her childhood days. What piqued Sarika's curiosity was that she often dressed her dolls in boys' clothes, preferring trousers and shirts to frocks and gowns. As a mother, Sarika felt it was her child's right to do what she wanted and did not question Tina about it..

Days passed uneventfully until September 12, 1975. The family received a bad news in the afternoon. Tina's paternal uncle was killed tragically in an accident, plunging the whole household in gloom. Friends and relatives flooded the house to condole with the family and to be with her grandparents who were inconsolable after losing a young son. He was just in his early forties. Tina was left confused, unable to cope with the loss of an uncle she was really close to.

After the cremation was over, Tina came back from her neighbour's house where Sarika had sent her in an effort to insulate her from the overpowering sense of grief at home. She wandered around feeling unhappy among crying and sobbing relatives. But there was no one to attend to her or listen.

Walking listlessly from room to room, she went into her deceased uncle's room on the ground floor in her house, hoping to catch the remnants of his love and warmth. As his widowed wife, her aunt, had moved upstairs to be with the rest of the family there was nothing left but the two couches covered in velvet. The emptiness gripped Tina, making her feel cold and helpless.

It wasn't easy even though, by and by, the rest of the household started picking up the pieces and moving on. Tina, now almost nine years old, found it hard to shake off her sense of discouragement.

Television helped somewhat to keep her mind occupied, so most of her time was spent watching her favorite programmes.

That's where it began....

At a particular moment, something made her stop while surfing channels at a particular scene in a movie. A couple was making love, with the camera panning really closely to capture each movement in fine detail.

Watching the flickering screen, Tina flashbacked to that fateful day when she had barged into her cousins' room and caught them watching a porn film. She had been horrified then.

Something seemed to have changed now. Fascinated, she continued watching till the scene changed.

Troubled by strange emotions, she left her room and went downstairs. The only room where her uncle had lived that no one used or rarely visited was empty as expected. Tina locked herself in, walked to the couches, pulled the cloth to reveal the two, purple couches, joined the two and lay down, marveling at the softness of the velvet.

Remembering the movie she had seen earlier, very slowly, she started exploring her body with her hands, touching each part gently, sighing as she explored what was most sensitive, almost losing herself in the thrill of it.

By and by, she became aware of soft knocks on the window. It seemed to have been going on for some time. Composing herself, she looked, and to her horror, Riya, the daughter of their household help, was looking in, her face flushed.

Hoping that the girl had not seen anything, Tina walked up to her and asked her to leave. Riya refused to do so. Boldly opening the window and looking straight into Tina's eyes, she said, "I will tell everyone about what you were doing if you don't let me in."

Scared, Tina allowed her to climb in and the two stood face to face. "Let us continue with what you were doing," Riya urged. "What do you mean?" asked Tina. Riya moved closer to touch her and say,

"Let's do it. It will be fun."

"Are you aware of what you are asking?" Tina questioned her again. "Yes, I have seen movies. I know what goes on," was the response.

Now Tina was totally under Riya's control and strangely unable to pay attention to her own will, Tina did what she was told. Riya guided her to the couch and helped her take off her clothes before touching her and urging her to do the same.

Both were lost in the act, understanding nothing but the pleasure they were getting out of each other, killing their loneliness somehow.

Chapter 5
Don't look back... ever

Tina was now virtually at Riya's beck and call, their secret meetings began late in the afternoon, when family members had settled in for a nap.

Much as she desired, Tina could not shake off the other girl. If she dared refuse to meet her, Riya would get rough, slapping her and often using force.

As Riya's mother was a house help and had very little money to fall back on, Riya lived in a small room provided by Tina's family. It was located close by, so she had easy access to the house.

Tina felt trapped, exhausted both physically and mentally, constantly worrying that her family would discover her dark secret.

Concerned to see her daughter retreating into her shell again, Sarika kept enquiring after her health.

To this, Tina had a stock reply: "Yes, I am well, but I just feel tired because of homework."

The rest of the family too remained mystified by Tina's behaviour, unable to understand why the little girl's sparkle had dimmed. But most of them were still learning to move on after the loss of her uncle so did not make too much of it.

And just when Tina had started thinking that she was sinking deeper into a deep, dark abyss, Tina's father Jayant sprang a surprise.

She was sitting in her mother's room talking to her when he walked in, looking excited. "What's going on?" Tina asked.

They were moving to Delhi. "We have decided and we have a lot to do over there and there is a need to expand the business," he said.

Hearing this, Tina knew that finally she had found freedom. Happiness bubbled within her. She jumped on the bed, yelling with joy.

Surprised to see her so joyous because they were afraid that the news would make her unhappy as she was very close to her cousins and aunts and uncles, her parents looked relieved, not knowing that their little girl had finally found a way out of her anguish because Riya would no longer be able to torture her.

As they had to move immediately because Jayant had to take care of the inauguration of the new business premises, he asked Sarika if she needed time to put things in order before joining him. Both were surprised, when Tina strongly said, "No, I want to go with you right now." Thinking Tina wanted to be with her father at any cost, Sarika relented.

Suddenly, it was as if a dark cloud had lifted from over Tina. Her mother wondered why it had happened, but then thought the child was happy that she would be away from a joint family and get her parents' undivided attention.

Tina also asked Sarika not to say anything to Riya's mother about their move. Sarika thought it was because the two were friends and would miss each other, but Tina was afraid Riya would get angry and tell everyone the truth.

They did not have to carry much anyway as the house they were renting in Delhi was fully furnished.

It was time to leave.

Next early morning at around 5 am, Sarika, Jayant and Tina left Dehradun after fond farewells to the family members. Though it was hard for all of them to say their goodbyes, they comforted themselves with the thought that the move was good for Jayant's business interests.

Everyone came out to the car to see them off. And as Tina opened the back door to settle in the backseat and glance out of the back window, she could see Riya standing behind the half open front door, looking angrily at her.

Tina turned her head immediately and, hugging her teddy bear tightly, looked straight ahead. The car started moving and she did not look back.

Chapter 6
A loved one leaves and a predator attacks

Delhi promised good times. The family settled down quickly in Janakpuri in a beautiful two-bedroom rental and Tina started going to a reputed school in the neighbourhood.

After much thought, Sarika also took up a job to support her husband financially.

Busy with new friends and studies, Tina slowly healed from her traumatic experience with Riya. As Sarika worked till about 7 in the evening, Tina spent an hour after school playing one sport or the other, which the mother approved as she was against children remaining confined indoors. Later in the day, Tina spent time with her landlady who lived on the ground floor of their house. The 55-year-old widow who had no children poured all of her love and affection on the young girl and took good care of her.

Time flew by and before they knew it two years had passed. Things, however, had taken a turn for the worse for Tina's father. His business was not doing too well and the sudden death of his father due to heart attack left them shattered.

Now 11 years old, Tina was mature enough to truly understand how much she would miss her grandfather, even as her family decided to relocate to Dehradun as Jayant, the eldest son of the family, was needed at home to manage his father's business affairs.

Another cremation within a few years from Tina's uncle's death weighed heavy on everyone's heart. Tina was in agony as she witnessed her father perform her grandfather's last rites. Her 80-year-old grandmother's tears brought forth a flood of emotion and as she hugged the elderly woman, Tina said, "Don't worry granny, I have come back to take care of you."

The death of the elderly patriarch brought its own troubles. The business started failing without his stewardship, disagreements and disputes over property issues arose as the family members fought for their rights.

Fed up, Tina's father broke away from his family with his share of money from the property and business and rented a house near her maternal grandmother's (Nani) home. .

During this time Tina had grown very close to Geeta, who lived close to Nani's house and was a year older than her. Geeta had two older brothers and they seemed friendly so Nani allowed Tina to go over to their house to spend time playing games or watching TV with them.

One day, when Tina was visiting, Geeta's eldest brother Jay suggested they play hide and seek, something that was eagerly accepted by the children. As Geeta was "seeker", who had to look for the rest of them, she counted up to 10 as everyone scattered looking for places to hide.

Jay and Tina hid in a cupboard.

Holding her breath, Tina waited to hear Geeta's footsteps when Jay's hand brushed against her. Thinking he had touched her by accident, because they were standing close to each other, Tina moved away, only to have it happen again.

And then, he really came for her, one hand urgently seeking her deepest parts, hurting her, causing her shame and the other clamping her mouth.

Traumatised by the brutality of the boy who had been polite to her all this while, Tina opened her mouth to scream but could not as Jay continued to torture her.

Even as Geeta seemed to take an eternity to come into the room where the two were hiding, the doorbell rang and Geeta's voice floated up, "Mom's here." Immediately Jay removed his hand and Tina ran out of the cupboard, and out through the main door.

Once back in Nani's house, she hid in the washroom sobbing, clenching her legs tightly together as the pain that Jay had inflicted became unbearable.

"It's my skirt, it's my skirt," was the thought that arose. Tina felt the skirt that showed her legs was the reason why she had been molested. She tore it off before standing under the shower and giving herself a good scrub.

By the time she had towelled herself and worn a pair of shirt and trousers, Tina's mind was made up. She wasn't going to keep quiet, no matter how scared she was of the repercussions.

The moment she got a chance to speak, Tina went to Geeta's house to talk to her about Jay's assault and the trauma it had caused her. "Please tell your mother about it, Geeta, so that he does not repeat this act with any other girl," she pleaded.

Geeta did not say a word and appeared to be in shock, which was natural because Tina had spoken out against the older brother she adored. But she did speak to her mother about it.

Her mother, with her very own orthodox and conservative views, however, refused to believe her precious son could do such a thing.

The first thing she did, was ask Tina to leave the house and to not come back again. No apologies were offered.

Sobbing again, she ran to her grandmother's home and locked herself in her room, crying her heart out.

Destiny had played a dirty game again with her, leaving her mind in turmoil.

Chapter 7

A mind in chaos

The next few days after the incident, Tina was numb. Even though she tried, she could not bring herself to talk to her mother about it as Sarika, also very conservative in her views, had earlier warned her not to play with boys now that she was growing up.

Tina knew her parents would raise hell if they found out what Jay had done to her. "Mum was right. I should have listened to her. This would not have happened," she berated herself again and again.

It was like being on an emotional rollercoaster. One moment Tina felt low and worse the next.

Wild thoughts plagued her. It was the skirt that had invited the attack. Maybe she was weak, which encouraged people to take advantage of her.

Tina could not stop this chaos in her mind, her self esteem was shattered into pieces..

There was no friend who could comfort her or help her.

Miserable, she decided against going to her Nani's house and facing the risk of running into Geeta or her family. So she told her mother that she preferred to stay alone at home as frequent power cuts at Nani's house distracted her from her studies.

Sarika was upset to hear this as she did not want to leave an 11-year-old alone in an empty house, so after discussing the matter with Jayant decided that Tina would be better off attending tuition classes after school.

Happy to get help with her lessons and also stay far away from Geeta, Tina now made up her mind to focus only on her studies and not think about anything else.

It was a good arrangement. Her tuition kept her busy and kept her from dwelling too much on the past.

Gradually, within the passage of two years, her grades improved, something her teachers lauded. Enthusiastic participation in sporting activities also helped her stay fit.

Now almost 13 years old, Tina, however, was beginning to feel the pangs of hormonal changes.

Despite opting for feminine attire she also did not feel good about her looks.

At school too Tina came in for some teasing from the girls because they said she had a flat chest. Sarika's insistence that she wear her hair short because of her hectic routine also did not help.

She was also increasingly noticing how the boys in her class paid attention to all of the pretty girls with good bodies and spoke to her only when they needed help with their lessons.

With her self-esteem at the lowest of lows, Tina started acting coy and doing all sorts of things to attract the boys' attention, but nothing happened. Her cousins too got back to calling her "Bro" for brother, forcing the girl to build a really negative image of herself.

Sarika found it difficult to handle Tina's problems despite trying to talk to her and to get her to smile again. Nothing was working. Tina's loneliness grew deeper by the day as she saw the girls in her class form tentative bonds with boys.

That was why, one day, at a family function, Tina took special care to dress up, wearing a red top and white trousers to stand out in the crowd.

Feeling happy after days, she was sitting in a corner and chatting with her cousins when a boy walked up to her with a friendly "Hi". Her response was friendly. She knew he was a friend of her cousin and thought he must have greeted her because their families were friends.

Once she was home, however, Tina was surprised to hear the landline ring late at night. Her parents were in their bedroom so she went to the living room to answer it. "Hello," a voice said softly. "May I know who it is?" Tina enquired. "Karan," was the response. "I just wanted to hear your voice," he said, and hung up.

It felt strange. For the first time in her life a boy had said something nice to her about her voice and not her studies.

Tina went to bed with mixed emotions and fell asleep deeply, not giving Karan's phone call much thought.

Chapter-8

The need to tell lies

Tina got up very early morning around 5am as she was still restless from karan's call last night.

Surprised to see her up and around, her parents asked if everything was all right. Though she said yes, in her heart Tina felt something was amiss. As she had time in her hands she went out for a walk, wanting to be close to nature and to clear her head.

It was summertime and the park near Tina's house was buzzing with activity as joggers did their rounds and children played happily. The freshness of the morning made her feel better and she started running, keeping up the momentum for half an hour before going all out of breath and collapsing on a bench.

The time now was 6 am and as she raised her

water bottle to her lips for a sip a boy appeared on the tracks and sat next to her. She turned to look at his face and her heart gave a little leap as she realised it was Karan.

Not knowing what to do, her first instinctive reaction was to get up, but when she walked away she heard Karan call out her name. "Tina, please sit down, just for five minutes," he pleaded. His presence was a surprise and she knew now that her discomfort in the morning had stemmed from his call last night. When she hesitated, he said, "Please don't jump to conclusions. I come here for a walk every day. I just saw you and came over to say hello."

Tina didn't know what she was expected to say so just replied: "Okay, I believe you," and went home.

She had to rush to get ready once she realised how late she was and had to run down to the dining table to hurriedly gobble down her breakfast. "What's up?" asked Jayant, who had already started eating. He was surprised that Tina had not said her prayers as she did every day before taking the first morsel. Sarika, who was serving, also looked up, which irritated Tina and she quickly finished her meal without replying and left the table.

This incident with Karan was disturbing for Tina as she had not handled a situation like this before. Try as she might she could not stop thinking about him, especially his eyes as they gazed at her. She hated expending all of her energies on it.

Picking up her bag, she said goodbye to her parents and boarded the bus. Karan was sitting in the front seats with her cousins and as she made her way to the back to an empty seat she knew the 10-minute ride would seem very long.

Not wanting to feel awkward, she kept mostly to herself in school and did not step out of class. Her emotions surprised her. All this while she had wanted boys to pay attention to her, but now all she wanted to do was run away from this good looking and intelligent boy instead of reciprocating the interest he showed in her.

Perhaps he's playing a prank, she reasoned. He could get any girl he wanted, why would he want to talk to her? Were her cousins encouraging him to make a fool of her? She thought she had a fairly good idea of what it took to make a handsome boy fall in love with a girl and believed she did not have any of those qualities.

When classes got over, Tina walked out of the school gates towards her tuition classes. Suddenly a shadow fell across her path and she looked up to find Karan standing in front of her. "What do you want?" she asked angrily. "What are you doing here? Why are you doing this?" She sounded shrill and desperate as she ended with, "You know my cousins will not like it."

Karan remained calm. "I think you are mistaken, I have not come here for you. I take tuitions too," was his reply.

Embarrassed, she mumbled an apology before going to her class. Two hours later, she decided to skip the bus and was walking home when Karan appeared again. Tina remained quiet, wondering what he would have to say this time. Though he fell into step with her, he too did not say anything for a few minutes before blurting out "I love you."

Shocked, Tina stopped on her tracks and looked at his face. Then, when Karan stretched out his hand to hold hers she recoiled and started running towards her house.

She could only sigh with relief once she made it to the front door without looking back. It had been very disturbing and she didn't want to think about it. but while changing her uniform something made her stop and look at herself. She was still the same girl with a flat chest. How could a handsome boy fall in love with her?

That evening, Tina struggled to study, unable to concentrate. Karan dominated her thoughts. She wondered what he was doing at that moment and if he had been upset with her reaction.

Unable to bear it anymore she called Shruti, one of her best friends who lived close by. "Come over," Shruti said, hearing the urgency in her voice.

Once there, Tina went to Shruti's room and closed the door for privacy, pouring her heart out to her before tears made it impossible for her to go on. Her friend was gentle with her, calming her down, trying to understand what was bothering her.

"Don't worry, I know Karan very well" she said, adding, "You have been hurt in the past but not all people are the same."

Shruti was also curious to find out why Tina was reacting so negatively to the situation, especially when she was always complaining about boys not being interested in her. "You should be happy if someone as handsome as Karan wants to be your friend," she said.

That's what I'm bothered about," said Tina. "What does he want from me when he can have someone much better than me?"

Adding that it was Karan's choice to pick someone he liked, Shruti, puzzled by Tina's expression, asked if she was hiding something from her. "I don't know," was the reply. "I want boys to be attracted to me to satisfy my ego but somehow I don't feel attracted to them. I don't want them to come close to me," she said.

"Has this happened because of your experiences in the past?" asked Shruti curiously.

"No, the past does not have meaning for me

now. All I know is that I don't want a boyfriend, Tina said.

Shruti nodded, thinking her friend wanted to focus only on her studies and did not want boyfriends to distract her.

"Please ask Karan to stay away from me," Tina pleaded.

"Fine, I'll do that," Shruti reassured her.

Thankful that her friend could help her, Tina gave her a hug.

Chapter 9
Did Tina lie to me ..

Conversations continued between Me and Tina

Absolutely engrossed in Tina's story, I took time to get back to earth after she suddenly stopped speaking. "What's wrong?" I asked as she kept quiet and looked out of the window with a faraway expression.

"It's quite late, you must be tired," I continued, just to get her to speak as the silence was getting awkward. "Yes, I think so, I must go now," she said abruptly.

Though my gut feel told me it was something other than tiredness, I smiled just to put her at ease.

As she got up from her chair and moved to the door to go to her room, Tina stopped suddenly to say, "Sunaina, I lied to my friend Shruti that evening."

"What lie are you talking about?" I asked.

"We will talk tomorrow, have a good night," she replied.

I shut the door and lay in bed recalling everything she had told me. What did she lie about? Why did she do so? There were numerous questions in my mind, but soon sleep overcame everything.

The alarm went off sharp at 7 am. Feeling lazy I decided to stay put in bed for a little while. Five minutes later, however, I was fully awake as my mobile phone rang.

It was Tina. "Good morning, Sunaina, when are we meeting today?" She sounded calm. Curious about what she had left unsaid the previous evening, I said I would meet her in an hour for breakfast in my room.

She was there on time and both of us enjoyed delicious idlis and sambar. "I know you are eager to find out more about Shruti," she said when we settled down to talk. I nodded.

"It was not that I was not attracted to boys. I was," Tina said, sighing. "Then what was the problem?" I asked. Her answer left me stunned. "I liked Shruti too."

Truth dawned. Tina was bisexual. She was attracted to both males and females, Karan and Shruti.

My first instinct was to recoil and move away from her. But then I realised I had behaved exactly how I would expect many judgemental people to act. It was wrong.

Organising my thoughts quickly I turned to her. "Now I understand what you are trying to tell me. But why did you hide it from me?"

Her reply was, "I didn't want you to judge me like others did."

"What's so terrible about it? It's human nature, isn't it? Our inclinations are sometimes not in our control. We are all unique and equal at the same time," I told her.

Her eyes welling up, Tina asked, "So, do you still want to know more about my life? About, what I went through?"

Yes of course, I replied, getting up to bring her a glass of water.

Chapter 10
Arrows fly thick and fast

Tina had lied to Shruti about Karan because she did not want to lose her as a friend. Her feelings were beginning to bother her. She was attracted to both boys and girls.

Karan was nice – so nice that she was afraid to acknowledge her love for him. Shruti evoked similar emotions too. Tina wanted to touch her and hold her close, but was afraid that Shruti would hate her for it and never speak to her again.

But in the middle of all of this, Tina had decided to not suppress what she felt for Karan and explore her feelings in depth. However, the next day at school, though she looked around for him he did not turn up.

There was, however, a pretty girl with him at the

tuitions and both joked and laughed before class even as he ignored her completely.

Taken aback by his behaviour, Tina wound her way home after classes, her mind preoccupied with the day's events. So engrossed was she with her thoughts that she did not realise Karan was walking behind her till he called her. Suddenly happy, Tina looked at him with a big smile, but her expression changed as he started talking to her.

It was poison. Karan said his friends had, had a bet with him to see if he could become friends with her and get her to speak to him. He had taken up the challenge, so all of this had been play-acting and he was telling her all about it as he had won the wager.

His words tore into her as he body shamed her, viciously pointing out each and everything about her that he thought was wrong, confirming every doubt she had about herself.

And then he was gone, leaving behind a pale and distraught Tina. Unable to go home in this state she rushed to Shruti's house and straight to her room, throwing her bag on the floor, flinging herself on the bed and bursting into tears.

It took Shruti everything to stop Tina from crying. She closed the bedroom door first as her parents were at home and she didn't want them to find out what was wrong.

Her soothing voice and kindness was balm to Tina's pain. Making her sit up in bed and offering her a glass of water, she wiped her tears with a handkerchief and cupping her face asked why she was in such a state. Sobbing, Tina hugged her tight, conveying her distress. Shruti attempted a guess. "Did Karan say something?"

Her cheeks touching Shruti's, their bodies close, Tina poured out details of her ordeal, tears rolling down her face.

Her heart going out to her friend and unable to figure out how she could comfort her, Shruti, still holding Tina, kissed her cheeks.

Bewildered, Tina looked into her eyes and kissed her back. Hungry for comfort, she clung to Shruti. Then, slowly, they caressed and kissed each other on their necks and faces before slowly and deliberately allowing their lips to touch.

Tina, her pain forgotten, let out sighs of delight as their bodies moved together and time seemed to come to a standstill… Until both froze when they heard Shruti's mother calling her.

Realising they had gone too far, both looked down, feeling embarrassed. Shruti held Tina's hand and apologized. "I am sorry, I don't know what happened, she said. Tina silenced her by putting her hands on her lips. "I love you," she told Shruti.

Their eyes shining, the girls went out of the room

and Tina left after exchanging loving glances with her friend.

No one noticed.

Chapter-11

Betrayal

It was routine now for Tina to go to Shruti's house after tuitions. As Shruti, like Tina, had working parents, both the girls were left on their own for a large part of the day.

Their relationship was getting intense and both enjoyed each others' company as they shared each others' interests in movies and books.

Then, it was time for exams in their respective schools. However, when the results were declared Tina was among the toppers while Shruti's performance was average.

This upset her parents, especially Shruti's mother Leela who did not like Tina at all but allowed the girls to spend time together as she had a busy schedule and did not want to leave her daughter alone. Both

Leela and her husband knew Tina's family too.

Tina's scores fuelled Leela's anger and she kept trying to convince Shruti that the other girl's influence was hurting her interests. "She has taken advantage of your naivety and gullibility, revised her lessons in her spare time and distracted you from your studies by coming over here," Shruti was told.

Now when the girls met, Shruti's tantrums increased as resentment against Tina kept building up. She knew her friend was very attached to her and had no one else to turn to so she became very dominating and authoritative.

Soon, Tina's phone calls were being ignored. Shruti responded negatively to everything she said. She also started befriending other girls in the colony.

Her heart breaking, Tina decided to meet Shruti in an effort to retrieve their friendship. She was home playing cards with some other girls. Hurt that she had not been invited, Tina sat down anyway, hoping for a break to talk to her friend.

Shruti enjoyed seeing Tina uncomfortable and upset, and started throwing disgraced comments at her about her clothes and boyish looks. Feeling her face getting red as a few girls started giggling, Tina got up to leave. Changing colours like a chameleon because she could not have her "victim" slip out of her clutches, Shruti asked her to take all that she'd said as a joke. "Don't take it seriously, sit down," she smiled.

Though upset, Tina stayed behind and joined the card game. This is not how friends behave. We have been together for three years and I love her. But her behaviour has changed, Tina thought.

It was late in the evening when everyone except Tina left. Both she and Shruti knew they had to talk about their relationship.

"Why are you doing this?" Tina came straight to the point when the two of them were alone. There was no one at home as both the girls' parents had gone out together for a wedding. Shruti chose not to answer. Desperate for attention Tina tried to grab her but Shruti pushed her away. Tina fell down and started crying.

Shruti, who had deliberately suppressed her emotions for Tina because of her mother's dislike for her friend and jealousy over her good performance in academics, again felt her heart go out to the weeping girl.

She apologised and helped her up and then gave her a kiss, which Tina responded to eagerly. Both hugged and talked till 10 o'clock at night before their parents returned and then fondly bade each other goodnight.

However, despite making up, Tina somehow failed to get her relationship with Shruti back on an even keel. It was like a few days of sunshine and then a lot of rain. After a few happy days, Shruti's behaviour turned toxic again. She developed a pattern of insulting Tina in front of other people and then making up for it by being overly affectionate with her.

A confused Tina did not know how to cope with this. Her studies were affected and grades fell drastically. So much so, even Shruti did better than her, much to Leela's joy and Sarika and Jayant's annoyance.

However, Tina's reaction to Shruti's grades was totally different from Shruti's. She was happy for her friend and congratulated her, which was not, however, received very graciously.

Things came to a head, however, very soon. One afternoon after school Tina was surprised to get a call from Shruti inviting her to a restaurant in town. She said she wanted her to meet someone. Tina agreed, just for the sake of old times and made her way there after tuition.

She entered the restaurant dressed casually in a shirt and trousers. Looking around she saw Shruti sitting at the corner table with someone else whose face was not very clear in the dim lighting.

Once closer to the two she saw the other person was Karan. Her heart in her mouth but hesitating only for a second to breathe deeply Tina walked to the table and allowed Shruti to grab her arm and guide her to a chair.

Angry at this unexpected encounter and blaming Shruti entirely for it Tina turned to her, tears in her eyes. "Why did you call me here? What are you doing with him?"

All of the negativity she had experienced with Karan welled up in her heart as she looked at his face. His smile gave nothing away but there was no regret or compassion in his eyes.

But then, it was not Karan she wanted answers from. Shruti was the one who had a lot of explaining to do.

Realising this, Shruti began: "Look Tina, I wanted to tell you something, but we have been fighting for the last few days and so I kept quiet."

As Tina looked at her quizzically, Shruti took Karan's hand in hers and said, "We are in love with each other."

Her heart pounding, Tina stared at them for a minute before picking up her bag and walking out of the restaurant, tears rolling down her cheeks.

All she knew was that she had been cheated by two people she had loved and one of them was her best friend too.

She knew the damage was irreparable and realised it would take her a long time to heal.

Back home, struggling to stay in control before her parents, she lied that she had eaten and did not want dinner, and only let the tears flow once she was in bed.

No one heard her cries.

Chapter-12
Blowing hot and cold

The next few days went by in a blur. Tina completed her routine, everyday chores like a zombie, worrying about what Shruti would tell Karan in case they took their relationship to the next level.

She and Shruti had been more than close friends and had shared a secret physical relationship. Would she tell Karan everything about it? How would Karan take it? Would he talk about it to everyone, even her cousins?

The thought made Tina's blood run cold. How would her friends and family react? Tina couldn't bear the thought of looking into her parents' eyes after that. How could she give them a shock like that?

Tina decided she needed to protect herself and

her reputation. Her class tests were starting and she wanted to focus completely on her studies so she decided to free herself from her fears and ask Shruti to not give away their secrets. So one evening after school on her way back home she dropped in at Shruti's house. The gate was open so it was easy to just walk in. "I'm going to have it out with her once and for all. She's playing with my emotions," Tina kept having an inner conversation with herself while gearing up the courage to ring the doorbell.

No one seemed to be around, which was surprising because Shruti was normally home at this time. Tina called out to her but got no response. Suddenly, however, she heard her name.

Turning around, she spotted her friend. But this was not the cocksure, as-mean-as-you-can-get Shruti. The girl was looking exhausted and sick. "Are you all right?" asked Tina? "Yes," Shruti said, obviously untruthfully. "Why have you come here?"

Tina did not beat around the bush. "Does Karan know about us?" she asked, repeating her question again till Shruti burst out with a loud "No."

"Then why did you do this to me? Why? We were such good friends," Tina said, sadly.

Shruti kept quiet, her eyes downcast. But Tina did not budge from where she was standing. She needed an answer.

Looking defeated but angry, Shruti screamed: "This is not natural. No one is going to accept it. We are girls and we can only have relationships with boys or it will be a disaster."

"How can you disregard my feelings?" Tina shot back. "If you are convinced about your beliefs, why did you get into a relationship with me?"

"Now I have ended it," replied Shruti, her shoulders drooping.

It dawned upon Tina then that Shruti had calculatedly and deliberately entered into a relationship with Karan because she was afraid of society tagging her as a "misfit".

As she turned to walk out of the house, Tina heard Shruti call out after her, "You are so selfish." Looking back, she replied, "You know better who behaved selfishly."

Shruti laughed sarcastically at this, retorting, "You see the condition I'm in? Does it not bother you? Has this so-called love you had for me vanished?"

Not willing to reply, Tina walked away.

The next morning Tina's parents suggested that she should call Shruti for a sleepover as they were going out of town and expected to be back late at night. Tina refused, saying "I have to study for a test so I don't want anyone to disturb me,"

The next day, however, when Tina felt a little

forgiving, she wondered how Shruti was feeling. Her gut feel was that somehow Karan was linked to her poor health and obvious unhappiness.

After much procrastinating she finally picked up her phone to give Shruti a call. "Hello?" Shruti was trying very hard to sound upbeat, but her voice gave her away. She was not doing well.

"How are you?" asked Tina.

"I'm okay," was the response.

"I am still concerned about you," Tina said, and closing her eyes tight as if to shield herself, said "I hope it's not Karan"

That brought on the tears. Hearing Shruti cry, Tina said, "Do you want to tell me everything?"

The answer was, "No, we just had a fight, nothing big." Then Shruti ended the call.

Tina looked at her phone. The friendship with Shruti had lost its charm entirely. "The girl is on another trip," she said to herself.

There was no way back to her.

Chapter-13
Rekindled hopes

Studies kept Tina busy even as she built walls around herself, interacting less and less with the outside world to the minimum.

She refused to open up to Sarika and Jayant too, knowing they were not as modern in their outlook as the parents of some of her classmates. They would not be able to accept her reality, which would then make her question her very own existence.

Her scores in exams too improved substantially. Immersing herself in her textbooks was the best way to compensate for Shruti's absence in her life.

Shruti and Karan were going strong and she often saw them together at the school canteen where she guessed Karan would have invited her.

It was difficult for her to see them laughing and

having a good time, but the former's truth was slowly making more and more sense to Tina. Society would not accept a relationship between two females. Only a boy could replace Shruti in her life.

At around this time Sameer a new student, joined Tina's class. He had changed schools and was very well behaved and intelligent, as his performance in the class tests proved. Often, during debates, Tina found his perspectives on certain topics very interesting and engaged in interesting conversations with him.

They had common interests, and soon both started looking forward to shooting the breeze together.

Months passed and their fondness for each other grew. As Valentine's Day approached all the students were asked to turn up in their favourite attire. Tina chose a beautiful white dress gifted by her grandmother on her birthday.

She looked in the mirror as she dressed up and thought she looked pretty. Her eyes were extraordinarily bright and her tresses, now long, were shining. She hoped Sameer would like what she was wearing and the thought of him made her blush.

She was hoping he would present her with a red rose on this special day.

There was a carnival atmosphere at school with everyone looking spectacularly good and excited about the celebrations.

It was a blessing that the school authorities were open minded and allowed boys and girls to mix freely without strict restrictions.

Tina looked around for Sameer but could not see him anywhere. Thinking he had taken leave that day, she went to the cafeteria feeling gloomy, ordered a cappuccino and then opened a book.

She was so absorbed in the story that she almost didn't notice a slight movement to her left. Looking up, she saw a beautiful red rose and a beautifully wrapped gift on her table.

Excited, Tina opened the parcel to find two beautifully crafted heart shaped fragrant candles. The name on the card was Sameer. Smiling happily, she looked around and found him standing in a corner.

"Thank you," she said, blushing happily.

"I love you," he said in return, making his surprise even more special. They sat together for a while, talking and laughing over their coffees before going back to class.

After school, at about 3pm, both went for a walk around the lake, holding hands and sharing stories of beautiful moments in their lives. Many young couples were wandering around the place, some with balloons, most of the women and girls holding roses. Sameer and Tina settled down on a ramp across the lake. As the cool breeze ruffled their hair, Sameer said "I love you" again, adding a question: "Do you?"

Tina's heart pounded and she could feel butterflies in her stomach. This was delicious, she thought, more beautiful than her relationship with Shruti.

"I want you, Tina," Sameer said, holding her now very cold hands tightly. Tearfully looking deep into his eyes, Tina said she loved him too.

Wiping away her tears he kissed her hands and then her lips. Overcome with emotion and unable to resist his touch Tina stood up. "Let's go back," she said, much to his surprise.

"Don't you like it here?" he asked. "No, I really do, but I'm afraid someone will see us here," she said.

As both parted with affectionate hugs, Tina couldn't stop smiling. Spending the evening with Sarika and Jayant in the living room she talked excitedly to them about everything under the sun. Both of them, not used to seeing her so full of life, felt very happy.

Tina went to bed after dinner at 10 pm and

was about to fall asleep when the phone rang. Her parents had retired to their bedroom so she ran to the living room to pick it up. It was Sameer.

"Were you missing me?" Tina asked, her face turning pink. "I could not sleep," he replied, and continued whispering sweet nothings into the phone. Her eyes closed, Tina listened, feeling a strong surge of desire for him.

Suddenly she heard her mother's voice. "Who's calling, Tina, are you still on the phone?" Startled, the young girl whispered a quick goodbye and tiptoed quietly to her room.

Sleep came swiftly as she snuggled under her blankets and fell asleep within minutes.

Chapter-14
The enemy strikes again

Tina was on cloud nine after meeting Sameer, the love of her life as she called him. Shruti was right, she told herself. The world loves a boy and a girl in love and accepts them, not a girl and a girl. This is normal.

Her happiness made her forgive Shruti for everything she had done to her.

Tina and Sameer were inseparable, sharing every little detail of their daily lives with each other, meeting each other's parents. Sarika and Jayant found him to be an intelligent, thoughtful person and good for their daughter as he helped her with studies and cheered her on if her performance in exams faltered.

Shruti knew about Sameer and though she and

Tina did not communicate with each other she wanted to meet Sameer once. The fact that a person she no longer liked had found a grounded, nice human irked her no end. She was envious of Tina and also unhappy because she had been fighting with Karan and he had tried to hit her. Tina had been right when she had seen her exhausted and miserable the last time she had come over to her house. Shruti was beginning to wonder if she had chosen the right person.

So when she bumped into Tina at a shopping complex one day, Shruti apologised to her for her behaviour, though it did not come from her heart. "I miss you, you know. It will be good for both of us if we forget what happened between us," she said.

Tina, soft hearted as always, melted. "Yes, you are absolutely right, Shruti. I have already let go of the negative memories."

Tina's voice reflected happiness and confidence. Something that had been missing before when she was with Shruti – which had allowed her to manipulate Tina.

"Can I come over to your school and have lunch with you in the cafeteria?" Shruti asked. "Let's talk and give our friendship a fresh start."

Shruti knew she was likely to meet Sameer if she went. So a few days later the three met up. Sameer already knew about her as Tina had told him they were friends, without going too much into the details.

Shruti looked stunning in a carefully chosen white dress. "Why is she dressed like that?" wondered Tina before she introduced the two of them. Soon, Shruti was chatting with Sameer with great interest, playing with her hair and giving him come-hither looks. Tina could not help but notice it, even as she and Sameer kept up their regular and humorous jokes.

"How's Karan?" Sameer's question surprised both Shruti and Tina. They had no idea that the two knew each other. Shruti went pale and mumbled about Karan being busy and having no time for her.

Observing Shruti closely, Tina now knew for sure that something had gone wrong between her and Karan. To cover up for her discomfort, Shruti now started flirting subtly with Sameer, laughing extra hard at jokes and asking him all sorts of personal questions.

"I hope you are having a good time with Tina. Hope she does not irritate you much," she changed the topic suddenly. Both Sameer and Tina felt awkward.

"Why should she do that," Sameer retorted angrily. "She is a lovely person."

"No, Tina gets insecure at times. That's why I asked you," Shruti laughed.

Now it was clear to Tina. Shruti was playing dirty games and could give away their dark secrets. Getting up from her chair, she told Sameer, "Let's go. We have a test tomorrow."

"Yes, you are right," he agreed, understanding from her disturbed look that something was wrong.

Shruti realised Tina did not want her to talk to Sameer and decided to create more trouble. "Don't worry, I'm not going to disclose anything."

That provoked an already tenseTina, who yelled, "What do you mean by disclose? What are you talking about? Do you think I'm afraid of you?"

As everyone in the cafeteria turned to look, Sameer was embarrassed and surprised by her sudden outburst. He had never seen Tina so angry. Her face was red and eyes tearing up.

Moving in for the kill, Shruti was all sweetness suddenly, asking softly, "What happened, Tina? Why are you shouting at me? I was just joking, you know me."

Sameer too took Shruti's side: "Yes, Tina. What happened? Are you okay? What did you think she was saying?"

Unable to handle the situation Tina stormed out.

Sitting there, Sameer wondered why she was reacting so angrily. He had known her for a year and was familiar with her maturity and sensitivity. But she had never been so, as he thought, unreasonable.

Shruti was now ready to add fuel to fire. "I am really sorry. I have really no idea why Tina behaved so strangely. Everything was said in jest, you know. Sorry again," she kept apologising.

Thinking she was being sincere, Sameer said, "No, please don't hold yourself responsible for her outburst."

Shruti dug in her claws deeper. "Sameer, I know you like her very much. She feels the same. I have known her for the past five years. She is a very sensitive girl, but sometimes she gets very insecure and suffocates the person she is with. I am not complaining. She is my best friend, but she is the only child of her parents and so demands attention all the time from everyone."

Reaching out to touch his arm, she continued, "I know you are a very sensible guy. I can understand you are doing your best to handle her tantrums, but I get disturbed."

Sameer was surprised by Tina's behaviour, especially as she had spoken warmly about Shruti and their friendship. Had she acted on the spur of the moment? Whatever it was, he was not used to it.

Shruti had succeeded in sowing doubts in Sameer's mind about Tina's behaviour.... that at times it could be unpredictable and unreasonable.

Sameer went back home with conflicted feelings and called Tina at 10pm, the time for their nightly conversation. No one picked up despite a number of attempts.

This angered Sameer. He felt Tina had to be made accountable for her behaviour and not embarrass him before other people.

Chapter-15
Seeds of disharmony

Sameer reached school fifteen minutes earlier than usual to talk to Tina. She was nowhere to be seen. No one knew where she was. Even her cousins were not in class when he went to look for them.

A tad worried, he thought of contacting Shruti. Sameer knew he could not rest until he found out where Tina was, and Shruti was likely to know. He knew where she lived because Tina had pointed out her house to him when they used to go on long walks.

Though classes were about to begin, Sameer ran out of the gates, hoping to quickly get the information he wanted and get back.

Leela, Shruti's mother opened the door when he rang the bell and introduced himself, explaining that he wanted to find out where Tina was. She said she had heard the news early in the morning that Tina's grandmother had died the night before.

As he thanked her and started walking out of the gate, Sameer heard Shruti calling him. Dressed in a T-shirt and pyjamas, Shruti appeared at the main door. She had missed school too. "Please come in," she said, showing him the way to her living room and introducing him to Leela.

Sameer gratefully accepted her mother's offer for coffee as she thought he looked exhausted, and just slumped on the sofa. Shruti reassured him that Tina would get back after her grandmother's funeral and started talking to Leela about how Sameer had started topping exams in Tina and Karan's school.

Leela was not too pleased about this good-looking, intelligent student being a close friend to the girl she disliked intensely. She was also impressed by the fact that he was the son of one of Dehradun's top and very wealthy lawyers. "You must come here more often," she said, giving him all of her attention and plying him with snacks.

Minutes turned to hours as the three chatted, Sameer now relieved to know where Tina was and very flattered with the attention he was getting from the two.

"Thank you for your wonderful hospitality," he said as he got up to leave, knowing he had no option but to go home as he had missed two to three important classes. Happy that her mother and Sameer had got along well, Shruti asked Leela what she thought about him.

"He's very nice," she said. "Try to be friends with him. He comes from one of the most prominent families in the city."

Shruti gave some thought to her mom's advice. Karan was still her boyfriend, but now she had come to realise that he was not good enough for her. What would make Sameer want to be her friend? She knew if she tried to hurt Tina again she would not take it lying down... but then Tina had no right to be with someone as wonderful as Sameer.

Shruti knew she would have to do something about them.

Tina returned to school after a few days, totally distraught after her beloved grandmother's death. She sat quietly in class not looking up even once. Sameer kept his gaze fixed on her. He expected her to inform him about her grandmother's death and was upset with her for not communicating with him.

She did not say a word even when they were in their tuition classes. Both had walked in separately and Tina chose a seat far away from him.

Sameer had started to lose patience but he also understood that Tina's grandmother's death must have been very traumatic for her as she was very close to her. So keeping his emotions in control he walked up to her after classes were over and asked if she would sit with him for some time in the cafeteria.

Tina was unable to say a word as both of them sat quietly, holding hands and drinking tea. Tears flowed from her eyes as Sameer watched and felt frustrated, knowing he could say or do nothing to comfort her except tighten his grip on her hand to let her know that he was always there for her.

"I'm sorry," she said finally, taking a sip of water. He knew what she meant and replied, "I understand."

Unaware of the lies that Shruti had been feeding him, Tina relaxed and smiled innocently.

He decided he would tell her later about his visit to Shruti's house. She had not said nice things about Tina, who, as far as he knew, was an innocent, forthright and an even-tempered person who could not be manipulated.

A seed of doubt grew in his mind. Had Shruti tried to influence him negatively against Tina? He decided to talk to her one more time to make sure.

Both of them finished their tea and after Sameer dropped Tina home he wondered if he should visit Shruti. Until he had discovered the truth he felt he could not tell Tina anything.

Once he reached Shruti's house, he found her and Karan chatting animatedly at the front door. She was taken aback because she wasn't expecting him and her newly awakened feelings for him showed clearly on her face.

This angered Karan who had been looking at her intently.

Sameer asked Shruti if she was busy and if they could talk. "No, no," she replied, "I was just seeing off Karan." Her boyfriend was not happy with what he had seen and glared at her, something that she completely ignored.

Karan had come to realise how petty and vicious Shruti could get but he was still possessive of her and held her hand to pass on the message to Sameer that she belonged to him.

However, since he did not want to create a scene he said his goodbyes to both and left.

Shruti invited Sameer in, telling him that they had all the time in the world to talk as her parents had not returned from work. Finding it a bit odd that she'd want to be alone with him, he told Shruti that he would come back later and went away.

Shruti had no idea why Sameer had come over, but she was glad that he had jotted down her phone number. Maybe he's interested in me, she thought, deciding to wait and watch and see if she had managed to drive a wedge between him and his girlfriend.

Chapter-16
Meltdown and misunderstandings

Shruti was getting ready for school when Sameer called. Leela answered the phone and greeted him warmly, enquiring about his health and family. "All good," he answered politely, before adding, "May I speak to Shruti please?" yeah sure,her mom replied back and gave the receiver to Shruti.

"Are you okay?" Shruti asked as he apologised, sounding very disturbed, for calling so early.

"No, I'm not," he said. "It's about Tina and what you said about her. Can you please explain?"

Shruti was careful. She did not want to overdo the criticism and put off Sameer. "Tina is a nice girl, but she has had issues since childhood. She gets insecure easily and gets very possessive of people in her life."

Sameer listened, not knowing what to say. His feelings for Tina were intense, but he wanted to be sure of her being the right girl for him. He was just not ready to be cheated in this relationship but he was actually confused now because for him Tina was entirely a different person from the one, Shruti described. At the same time, he knew that Tina and Shruti were best friends since their childhood. So, his mind was not allowing him to ignore this fact also. Sameer was all lost now in his thoughts ,then out of sudden Shruti's evil mind injected a new thought. She said, dont worry, I can understand your emotions, why dont you come to my home tomorrow after school. You can see yourself whether I am saying truth or not. Confused Sameer got agreed though he knew he was doing wrong but all he wanted truth.

Next morning, he was very quiet in school the following day though Tina sat next to him. "Is everything all right? She asked."

"Yes. I am just worried about the exams next month. It's just exam stress," he replied.

Tina nodded. Her thoughts were elsewhere too as she had brought big paper bags full of her clothes and stationery items for Donation Day, which she did every year to help the students in need..

This gesture touched Sameer and doubt Shruti again, but he still couldn't shake off the doubt that because he still wanted to give a chance to Shruti to prove whatever she said about Tina.

When school got over he told Tina he could not walk her home as he wanted to study in the library. Then waiting for 10 minutes after she had left he walked quickly to Shruti's house hoping no one would spot him.

Shruti, who was waiting for him all dressed up again in a pretty pink wrap and top, ushered him into the living room. Soon, back with steaming cups of coffee for both of them she settled down comfortably in the couch next to him, saying "Okay, now what did you want to talk about?"

Sameer had just started questioning her about Tina when the doorbell rang. He could hear a lively "Hi, come in," from Shruti as she ran to open the door. Then, much to his surprise, Shruti entered and Tina followed her.

As he stood up awkwardly, he saw Tina's face go white. "What are you doing here? You said you would be in the library and now I see you here?" She was getting angrier. "You lied to me, you cheated. You did not drop me home and now you have come to meet Shruti? What's going on? Are you two dating?"

Tina was crying, remembering when she saw Shruti and Karan together at the restaurant. Slowly, losing control over her mind, she started picking up books, magazines, an ashtray, whatever she could grab, and started throwing them at Sameer.

Shruti tried to stop her, Sameer was shocked with Tina's meltdown, not knowing how she had been pushed this far by Shruti. He was also angry with Shruti for inviting Tina as Shruti already knew that he had come to discuss a sensitive issue. "Stop, stop, stop," he shouted at Tina, running to her and forcing her to put down the brass idol she had picked up.

Then, looking sternly at Shruti, he said, "Why is she here? Why didn't you stop her at the door?"

Hearing this, Shruti realised she could have made a very big mistake by trying to manipulate Tina and Sameer against each other. Not knowing what to do, she directed all the blame at Tina. "Look at her losing control and behaving like a child. This is the real Tina, the one who does not trust the person she is with, who keeps creating misunderstandings and blaming people for things they haven't done."

She continued, looking at Sameer: "What have we done? We were just talking when she came in and started yelling at us. I invited her in because I thought we could sit and chat together like grown-ups."

Sameer had enough of this drama. He picked up his bag and started walking towards the door.

Tina, who had come to her senses by then, tried to follow him out. "Sorry, sorry," she wept. "I had absolutely no idea that you were visiting and was very angry to find that you had chosen to spend the afternoon with her. I didn't know what to do."

Sameer turned to her and held up his hand. As she stopped on her tracks, he shook his head, looked sadly at her and left.

A wave of emotion engulfed Tina. She did not want to lose Sameer. There would be no meaning in her life if she did.

Bursting into tears and looking with eyes full of hate at Shruti, she too ran out...

Chapter-17
Into darkness

Entering class the next day was like getting into a torture chamber. Tina was in early hoping for the chance to speak to Sameer, but he chose to ignore her, walking to his classes with a bunch of his friends and changing his seat next to her for another one.

The final exams were approaching so the entire class was super busy,, everyone was discussing the "difficult" portions of the syllabus. Sameer too talked anxiously with a few of the toppers, some of them girls. He did not look at her even once.

Tina waited for him at the cafeteria for their regular meeting place, but Sameer didnot come there. Tina picked her bag and entered her class. She was shocked to see Sameer's behaviour.

Just overnight, within 24 hours, he seemed to

have changed and become a different person. The girls were delighted that he was paying attention to them even if it was to discuss physics or chemistry. Earlier he had eyes only for Tina.

Tina felt quite lost and lagged in her lessons, forgetting her answers and getting pulled up by her teacher.

By the end of the day she had, had enough. When the bell rang she ran out and tried to hold Sameer's hand when he had started walking home. He shook her off and asked her to behave and "not cross limits."

Tina, however, didn't give up. She kept apologising as she followed him and he seemed to be listening.

However, at one point he stopped, turned around and told her that he was going to Shruti's house.

"Why?" she asked. "You know where our relationship got spoilt because of Shruti and now you are doing this to me?"

He could see her getting angry again, and he remembered Shruti talking about her "insecurities and possessiveness." "Yes," he said. "I am going to her house because her mother has invited me to lunch."

Tina gave him a long, hard stare and walked off.

At Shruti's house, Shruti's mother, Leela prepared herself all lunch, serving Smeer, biryani, chicken lababdar, phirni and other delicacies. They seemed to be really hitting it off, laughing and joking with each other till the car sent to pick him up arrived.

Both mother and daughter stood at the gate and waved till he was out of sight.

As Sameer drove past Tina's house he saw her standing outside the gates and their eyes met briefly. She was still in her uniform.

As the car vanished from sight Tina went into the house. Her parents had yet to return from work so she decided to take a shower. The tears would not stop as she stood under the warm spray, going over the day's events.

Sarika and Jayant returned by the time she came out of the bathroom. Her eyes were still puffed up from crying and she looked really pale so Jayant asked if she was unwell. "Did you get low scores in the test?" was his next question.

"Dad, I'm just not feeling well. I want to sleep. Can I?" Tina asked.

Hugging her close, he kissed the top of her head and said, "Okay. You need rest, but please eat something."

Blaming exam stress for her low spirits, Sarika made a sandwich for her and sent her to bed. But even then Tina could not sleep and kept tossing and turning.

At 10pm, when her parents had retired for the night, Tina tiptoed to the living room to call Sameer. Each unanswered call was like a blow to her heart, but she kept trying, wanting to hear his voice desperately.

Finally he picked up, his voice low but angry, saying "I'll speak to you tomorrow. People are getting disturbed by the ringing of the phone," and hang up.

Tina stood alone, in the dark, for a long time, just holding the receiver, listening to the dial tone.

Chapter-18
Trying hard to hold on

The next morning Tina combed her hair till it shone. She let it loose, the way Sameer liked, and knew she looked good.

Waiting for him at the cafeteria with a cup of coffee she saw him ride up on his new motorcycle – something he had been asking his father to get him for months.

Much to her joy, that morning, Sameer came right up to her table and sat down as if nothing had happened. Before Tina could say anything, he spoke "Look Tina, I know you are upset. I was upset too but now I am fine. We are about to give our final exams that are crucial for both of us. I know you want to top the class and so do I. So it would be better if we took a break from each other and concentrate on our studies. I hope you understand

and I expect such maturity from you."

Tina was speechless. She had been up all night thinking of things she would say to him. Was this the only thing left for him to say? She thought they would go for a walk and she would clear her stand to remove all the misunderstandings between them. She had imagined that he would tell her he loved her and apologise for being so cold and distant.

How cold and clinical he sounded! How different from the boy who was so protective of her! There was no affection in the way he looked and spoke to Tina. Everything was cut and dried now..

Who was this person? Her eyes welling up, Tina turned her face away to compose herself. He faltered for a second at the thought of her in pain.

As he reached out and touched her hand, its familiar warmth weakened his resolve to distance himself from her. "I do understand you," he said. "And I want you to know I will be around."

That was all Tina wanted to know. She let out a sigh of relief to know that their relationship was not damaged irreparably and decided to let him be as he was.

In the days that followed both got busy with studies as their exams were about to start. Tina did observe Sameer on and off in class and during tuitions, missing their intimacy at times, but it was not easy figuring out what she was feeling? Was it love or just a deep fondness for someone special? She did not know.

For Tina, Sameer and her education were both important, but she was wise enough to understand that this was not the time of compromise with her studies and so tried to detach as much as possible from her feelings for the boy who meant so much to her.

The stress, however, was intensifying for her. Unlike Sameer, Tina could not completely take control of her thoughts and found it difficult to concentrate. Studying day and night and then struggling to remember everything left her with no time to eat healthy and get some rest. A night before the exams she called Sameer to wish him luck but no one answered despite several attempts. Anxious and unhappy she walked to her room and suddenly felt everything go black.

When Sarika came to check up on her before going to bed she was horrified to see Tina lying unconscious on the floor and immediately called Jayant for help. Both splashed water on her face and rushed her to hospital after she regained consciousness.

After a thorough examination the doctor told her parents that Tina had been stressed out. Sleeplessness as well as weakness because of her poor diet had sapped her of all energy. He said she had to be put under observation. When they told him about her exams the next day he said she had to miss it.

As she was under sedatives Tina woke up at 10am the next day harnessed to an IV drip. Her parents, who had been waiting all night in the lounge came in and hugged her. The fact that she was missing her exam that day had not registered. "Don't worry papa I am fine," she told Jayant as he stood next to her bed and patted her on the head. Hearing this, Sarika bent down and gently kissed her on her cheeks.

Just then the doctor came in. "How are you doing?" he asked. "I am good," she responded so sweetly that he could not help but give her a hug and say, "Don't worry about your exam. Health is a priority. You can re-appear for your exam after some time."

Hearing this, Tina jumped out of bed, IV still attached, insistent on going to school. Her parents held on to her for dear life as she was still too weak to walk. "Please let me go, mom, dad, this is my last year in school. I won't get good marks or get into a good college," she pleaded, but they were having none of it.

Then, when she knew she would not be able to get her way, she lay down and went to sleep as the sedatives had yet to wear off.

The hospital released her by the evening. Tina was quiet at home. As Sarika was in the kitchen cooking, Jayant sat by her bedside and comforted her by telling her that she could reappear for the exam after a few months.

"Now relax and focus on your health first," he said, taking her hands in hers. Even then, however, Tina remained worried, thinking about all the entrance tests to colleges she was going to miss till she reappeared for the paper.

And then there was Sameer. He would also go away, probably to another city if he got admission elsewhere. The thought was too much for Tina and despite Jayant and Sarika's protests she went to the living room to make a call. "It's just a friend," she told them. "I have to ask him about the paper."

This time Sameer picked up the phone. "Hey, where were you?" he asked, extraordinarily cheerful. She was surprised at his lack of concern. "I was in hospital, had a blackout last night and the reason was too much stress."

The reaction she got from him was very different from what she expected. "Oh, that's too bad. You take care." There was no concern for her, no detailed questioning about her health, nothing. "I have to go now," he said and hung up.

Walking slowly back to her bedroom, she lay down with a sigh, knowing sleep would take a long time coming. He didn't care after all, did he?

It was no use moping. Tina decided to focus on getting better and write the rest of the papers that fortunately had long breaks in between. She was determined to do well despite the health setbacks.

Chapter-19
Mistaking lust for love

School was abuzz with excitement on the last day of the exams. Tina took special care with her clothes and applied kohl to her eyes – which Sameer had always liked.

They waved to each other before the bell went off for the paper distribution.

Tina had studied hard so she was very happy with her performance in remaining papers. Thanks to Sarika and her will power she had also managed her diet and sleep very well. She wrote her exam quickly, marvelling at how simple it seemed to her, and handed the paper to the teacher before walking out.

Finding Sameer waiting for her outside the class made her happier and both discussed the paper animatedly on their way to the cafeteria.

All this while, as they ordered their coffees and sat down at their favorite corner, Tina waited for Sameer to tell her how he planned to spend the vacations with her before his hunt for college began.

The news then that he was leaving on a trip that very night with friends came as a shock. "We planned it before our exams. I am so excited. It will be good fun. Do you also have some plans?" he asked her.

All Tina could muster up then was a fake smile. She was hoping to spend some quality time with him and here he was, off on a trip with friends. Why hadn't he discussed it with her?

"That's great. You will have great fun with your friends," she said, sipping her coffee. Even though she had yet to finish it, Sameer got up from his chair to bid her goodbye. "I'm sorry I have to rush. I still have a lot of packing to do. Bye."

She sat for a while, mulling over Sameer's behaviour. However, not wanting to pass on any negative energies to the relationship in which she had invested her heart and soul Tina waited for him to return.

He had said he would be back in a week, but after 10 days when she did not get a call she telephoned to find out where he was. A male voice answered, very similar to Sameer's, but when she bombarded him with questions about the trip the person at the other end of the line identified himself as Sky, Sameer's elder brother. "Sameer is not at home. May I know your name?"

Tina responded, requesting him to ask his brother to call back. "Certainly," he responded before the call was disconnected.

Tina was not sure how Sameer would react as she had never once spoken to any of his family members. Well, if he gets angry I will apologise, she reasoned.

But a week passed without any messages. Losing patience she called again, to hear Sky's voice. He identified her immediately, asked her to wait and called his brother.

Sameer sounded annoyed when he realised it was Tina. "Why did you call? Didn't I tell you I was travelling? I have been very busy after that and have no time for phone calls," he said.

As a long silence greeted him, followed by sobs, Sameer realised he had unnecessarily hurt Tina when a gentle explanation would have done. "I am sorry. I knew I should have called you but I have been really busy filing applications for various colleges."

Then, responding to her suggestion that they meet up, he said, "I am still very busy, Tina. Please try to understand." However, when she coaxed and cajoled he relented and said he would come to her house in the afternoon and hung up.

The gloom lifted instantly. Tina, who still found Sameer's behaviour strange, decided to really use the one chance she had with him to restore their relationship.

Next morning, after her parents left, she spent the day reading books before making pasta for Sameer. Then, setting the house in order she wore a pretty blue dress and waited for him to come around.

Sameer was dressed casually, unlike before when he took extra care with his appearance. Both of them sat next to each other on the couch as he excitedly recounted the adventures he had on his recent trip.

Suddenly, the atmosphere changed. He looked into her eyes and Tina realised with a start that their bodies were almost touching. Then Sameer took her hands in his own and put her palms on his heart, which was beating really fast.

Since she had not been with him for quite some time Tina felt a little shy. Sameer then pulled her on to his lap and started kissing her and she melted in his arms.

This was a different Sameer, more passionate, taking total control of her body.

Then he asked her to show him the way to her bedroom. "No," Tina said.

"Don't you trust me?" he asked?

"It's not that. I'm not ready for it. It's not right" she said. But he was not listening. "Please, I want to just hold and kiss you and feel closer to you," he said.

Unable to fight, Tina showed him where her room was. He grabbed her hand and pulled her inside.

She felt a moment of panic as he shut the door and made her sit on the bed, but she again forgot herself when he started kissing her all over.

Soon… Reality struck when she felt herself being pushed down and his hands, now rough, tearing off her clothes. "Enough," she shouted. "Stop." But he was not listening. Then, as she started screaming, he took her pillow, put it on her face, and forced himself on her, not bothering how much he hurt her.

When it was over he got up from the bed and asked her to "straighten up."

Tina was in shock. "Why did you do this to me?" She wept. "This was my way of showing you how much I love you," he said. "Don't worry, nothing will happen. You are on your period as I can see. You are a science student and know it will not make you pregnant."

"You forced me," Tina was not having it, even

though her heart was breaking because she now knew there was no love in that act, only lust.

'Tina, don't overreact. It just happened. I had made no plans. I couldn't resist you. You were looking so pretty. Please do not misunderstand me. Take a shower. Freshen up. You'll feel better," he said.

Then something strange happened. Tina saw him looking at her study table where she had kept all the cards and gifts he had given her. He got up and picked all of them. "Why are you taking them?" She asked.

"To save myself," he replied. And when she looked at him questioningly, eyes wide with surprise, he explained "I have written my name on them and bought these gifts for you. I don't want your parents to know what I'm doing in your life. Parents don't understand," he said, turning towards the door.

It was almost as if he was wiping off traces of a crime. She simply could not accept the clarity of his thought process, even as she was a bundle of emotions. As Tina followed him out to the living room she saw him put the cards and gifts in his bag and get ready to leave.

"Don't go. Stay for a while," she pleaded. "Whatever happened today should not have happened. How will I face my parents? How will I face myself?"

"It happened naturally," he replied. "All I know is that we love each other and I feel I have rights over you. Don't I?"

Tina did not reply. She was in pain and knew Sameer was responsible for it. He walked towards the main door, saying, "I'd better go, your parents can return anytime. I will call," and went away.

Tina went to the bathroom, and as hot water cascaded over her she wondered if she had been raped. There was blood on the floor. And as it flowed out with the water she closed her eyes and screamed.

But there was no one to hear her.

Chapter-20
Getting over heartbreak

It's not easy to heal from a heartbreak and often you are fooled into thinking you can rekindle a friendship and things will be as good as before.

But with Sameer that was not to be. He simply disappeared from Tina's life, not answering her calls or bothering to stay in touch with her.

Tina processed everything quietly, not wanting to believe in reality, hoping against hope that everything would get back to normal.

She was quiet and withdrawn again, locking herself in her room and brooding for hours. Her parents took her to therapists but it was very difficult to get her to open up.

They diagnosed her with depression.

Days passed, the urge to connect with Sameer

would take over at times, making her think she was going mad. There were times when she planned to go to his house to confront him with what he had done to her. Then she backed out thinking it would create unnecessary drama.

It took her time to pick up the pieces. Students who had been in her class were now studying for entrance exams for various institutions or joining colleges as she prepared to reappear for the exam she had missed. She had also begun venturing out of her home a couple of times to run errands for her parents. A thought had sprung up in her mind. Perhaps life could get back to normal again.

But achieving normalcy was not that easy.

Shopping at a market near Shruti's house one day she saw Sameer's motorcycle parked near the gate. There was no way in which she could forget the registration number. Standing rooted to the spot she did not know what to do… until she spotted Sameer and Shruti together. They were laughing and walking out of the gate.

Both of them hesitated when they saw her. Then Sameer walked up to her with a "Hi Tina." Then, seemingly not making much of the situation he started his motorcycle and rode off with a "Bye" to Shruti.

Weak and trembling, Tina could only stand there helplessly till she felt Shruti's touch on her arm. Memories of the friendship they had shared stopped her from turning her back on Tina, who was not looking good at all.

"Are you fine?" Shruti asked. That shook Tina out of her stupor and she buried her face in her shoulder, weeping helplessly. Shruti took her by the hand they soon reached Tina's home. Her parents were as usual still working so Shruti went into the kitchen and got her a glass of water, patting her shoulders while she dried her tears.

"Are you having an affair with him?" Tina asked bluntly. "No, he had just come to see me," was the reply. Shruti could not find it in her to be angry with this broken girl. She knew something terrible had happened to her and Sameer was responsible for it. He had obviously cut Tina out of his life completely.

"Wait a minute, did you know he is going to Delhi? He is joining one of the top colleges there."

"No," replied Tina. "He can't do this. He promised," she stammered, panic stricken.

Shruti understood what was happening. Tina was too deep into this to let Sameer go. Her hands were shaking and eyes glazing over. Glancing around she saw tablets on the bookshelf. "Are you taking medicines?" she asked.

"They are antidepressants," Tina replied. Shruti gave her one and sat with her till Tina calmed down.

They kept talking. When Shruti asked if she loved Sameer, Tina said "Yes," adding, "are you hiding something from me?"

Unable to take the shock when Shruti confessed that they had, had a physical relationship Tina had a panic attack. Shruti was forced to call Sarika and Jayant, who rushed home and took their daughter to hospital.

Shruti called Sameer when she got back home. "So you cheated on me too?"

Knowing he could not wriggle his way out of the situation, Sameer confessed. "It was just infatuation. I realised this when I met Meesha in Delhi. Believe me, Shruti. I thought Tina was the love of my life, and even when she had those meltdowns I tried to make it work. But when I met Meesha, who is joining my college too, I knew she was the one for me. We have a different level of compatibility. Please ask Tina to forgive me. She should focus on her health first."

After the call ended Shruti realised how much she had wronged Tina. To see the former bright and happy girl on antidepressants, on the verge of a disastrous breakdown had come as a rude wake-up call for her. Shruti realised she had been largely responsible for her friend's mental health issues, taking Karan from her first, then brainwashing Sameer to break up with her to have an affair with her instead.

She was grown up enough to realise that she had wronged Tina. No one had the right to destroy another and sooner or later the perpetrator would have to pay a price for it. Shruti had also developed strong feelings for Sameer and hearing him talk about Meesha hurt her badly too.

Maybe I deserved it, Shruti told herself.

She knew that the only way she could redeem herself was by building bridges with Tina, in whatever way she could. It would not help Tina but at least it could give her some comfort, Shruti reasoned.

She went over to Tina's house when she heard that the young girl was getting better. Holding her hand, she affectionately asked how she was feeling. "Improving," was the dull reply.

"Can you still trust me?" Shruti questioned her, tears in her eyes. "I already did," Tina smiled, pleading, "Shruti please tell me the truth. I can read your eyes. Don't worry, nothing will happen. I won't scream or shout. I don't have the energy, I am already broken."

"Sameer has a new girlfriend in college," Shruti blurted out.

Tina looked resigned but not too surprised or disturbed. "What's her name? Is she very pretty?"

"It's Meesha," Shruti said. "Both have been together for the last three months."

Seeing Tina in pain, she added, "I am very sorry."

"Why are you sorry?" Tina asked. "It was a fragile relationship and so it broke."

Shruti was amazed at her reaction, but Tina was finally accepting the truth. What was love for her was lust for Sameer. He used people. He had raped her.

Tina knew she was better off without him.

Chapter-21
A wonderful surprise

Tina moved on. She knew she had to if she wanted to live her life to the fullest. Sameer had taught her the worst lesson of her life, but it was a valuable lesson. She had learned how harmful it was to depend on another person for one's happiness. It never worked that way.

Though the past did come to haunt her one way or the other sometimes, Tina immediately moved focus from all the negativity and concentrated on healing herself.

She did not call Sameer again or seek answers from him. Closeted in her room, she studied hard for the one paper that remained and cleared it with very good scores.

Luckily, a local private college accepted her and

soon she was busy with classes, once again excelling in studies.

Three years passed, Tina was in final year and quite popular among the students as she was a bright student and was also always ready to help others.

As her father's business was doing well, they moved to a larger house in another part of town. Before she left, Tina said her goodbyes to Shruti, thankful that she was no longer interested in delving into past memories.

Tina personally supervised the décor of her room, getting the walls done up in turquoise and pale blue, her favourite combinations. There was room for everything – her books, music, material for new hobbies and sports equipment.

Soon, thinking that rentals would add to their income, Sarika and Jayant got new tenants for the upper floor. They were really nice people who got along very well with them.

Towards the end of the final year and to celebrate some of her achievements in college, Tina threw a party for friends, a carefully selected trustworthy bunch. Her tenants were invited too.

She was happy and radiant, receiving people that evening. Her tenants were welcomed warmly and Tina was surprised to see them bring along a guest, Alisha who was about Tina's age and her tenant's sister. She had come to Dehradun to do a diploma course and was very friendly. The party was great fun, with lots of chatter and laughter. Alisha and Tina bonded really well and soon both were going to the movies and on shopping sprees.

Tina had started to look forward to their outings. But one night, a very vivid dream about her and Alisha sharing intimate moments served as a warning. It made Tina realize that she was getting attracted to the young girl. However, given her past history, she was against setting herself up for heartbreak this time and decided to maintain distance from Alisha.

One evening her tenants went out for a wedding with Sarika and Jayant. Tina was studying so she was surprised when Alisha turned up with paranthas and a cauliflower and potato dish that she had cooked. "Let's have dinner together," Alisha said brightly.

As both sat down to dinner, Alisha removed her dressing gown. She looked rather fetching in her white satin nightsuit and Tina caught herself staring. Noticing her look, Alisha asked if anything was wrong. "No," Tina said, "You are looking rather nice. White suits you."

"Thank you," Alisha blushed. "You are looking great too." Both laughed and suddenly Alisha got up from her chair and hugged Tina tight, saying, "I really like you."

Her heartbeat accelerating, Tina didn't know

what to do. She didn't want anything to happen, but Alisha's sweet face looking up at her adoringly was too much to take and she bent down and kissed her on the lips.

The pleasurable feeling that hit her when Alisha kissed her back evoked strong memories of the past. She had lived for years without love and yearned to continue what Alisha had started.

Suddenly, Tina's mobile phone rang when she had started unbuttoning Alisha's shirt. She came down to earth abruptly and picked it up. I stopped at the right time, she told herself, while answering her mother, who had called up to ask if she had eaten.

Walking back to the dining table, Tina looked at Alisha and buttoned up her shirt, saying "I'm sorry, I can't do this."

This upsetted Alisha and she collected the bowls of food, left unfinished, and went upstairs.

Tina understood how she was feeling, but she was not in the state of mind to get close with someone again, especially a girl.

She had started getting worried about her feelings. "Am I bisexual? These questions had started to plague her as she was getting older.

A few days later when Tina wanted to go to an art exhibition she went upstairs and rang the bell to find out if Alisha was interested in going. Her sister answered the door and said that Alisha had left for her hometown Ludhiana early in the morning.

Did her own behaviour lead to this, Tina asked herself. But there was nothing she could do about it. She called Alisha later just to find out how she was doing, but the other girl did not answer.

After college Tina took some time to finalize her career options and was lucky to land a seat in a business management course at a prestigious institute in Delhi. It was quite an achievement as she was the only one from her college to get in.

Moving out of home was not very easy, but it was exciting being in Delhi with its special metro buzz. Tina got a room at the university hostel and did not find a minute to spare once classes started.

The only problem, however, was that she came from a middleclass family while most of the other students were from moneyed backgrounds, flaunting their wealth, the big international brands in clothing, accessories and cars. It did not matter at first but then Tina started getting affected by all the talk about eating in fancy restaurants or holidaying abroad. Most of her friends had boyfriends – many of them very good looking men from rich families – and so could not spend their spare time with her. She had to spend many lonely hours by herself in the hostel when it emptied out on weekends.

Again her self-esteem was impacted, especially now that Sarika and Jayant were not around to give her their love, care and attention. If only I had a friend, I would feel myself lucky enough, Tina told herself. Days passed on.

One Saturday a young man came to their hostel to meet his sister Jassi, on a Saturday when she had gone out for lunch. As Jassi was her roommate, Tina had to go down to the waiting room when the guard called to talk to the visitor.

"Hello," said Tina, as the tall, handsome man got up from the sofa once she entered, his hand outstretched. "Hi, I'm Akash, Jassi's brother," he said smiling. "Yes I know," Tina said with a smile. "She has told me about you but unfortunately she has gone out for a while."

"I just called her," he said, "I wanted to surprise her but she surprised me instead."

Both of them laughed when he said that. Though he dressed well and was obviously moneyed, Tina felt at ease with him. She decided to take him to the canteen for snacks as she knew he would be hungry as he had just flown in from Lucknow.

They had an interesting conversation. Aakash was a nice person working in the human resource department at a multinational company in Lucknow. He had a great sense of humour and also liked Tina's simplicity and the care she took of him in

Jassi's absence.

Soon, he took her leave and left as he had to leave town early in the morning the next day. Tina had a spring in her step. "How nice it was to meet a man who made me laugh so much," she thought. "He really made my day and went back to her room.

Now, Two years in the management course passed almost in the blink of an eye. Tina was about to complete the programme and was furiously burning the midnight oil for the exams that were starting in a month.

She had just turned 23 and her parents had started looking around for a suitable husband for her. However, all that Tina was interested in was work. Matters of the heart made her uneasy. There were still times when she woke up in a sweat with vivid dreams of Alisha and her holding each other, making love.

It upset her but she could never gather the courage to see a therapist who could diagnose her condition and help her. Society would never accept it. "It has to be a job first and then marriage and family," she told Jayant and Sarika.

After clearing her exams Tina started applying to various multinationals for jobs and soon got a call from a Mumbai-based company for a human resources profile with an excellent salary package.

Her parents were not too happy. They wanted her to get married and settle down and did not approve of her living and working on her own in a place like Mumbai.

Tina, however, told them that she needed time to make up her mind. Now more or less sure of her bisexuality, being with a man or a woman for the rest of her life was beginning to scare her. It was a secret only, she knew and she was not ready to share it with the rest of the world because of the stigma attached to anything unconventional that went beyond the acceptable man-woman norm.

Mumbai was more exhilarating than Delhi. Tina loved her posh two-bedroom apartment that her company allotted her and found her job really interesting. Her bosses too were very happy with her performance.

Soon, after a couple of months in the big city, she was chosen for an award and was going to be felicitated by the CEO, AK Bhasin at a five-star hotel in Delhi.

Very excited, she shopped around for a suitable dress for the event and bought herself a full-length classy black dress with a top designer label.

On the day of the award ceremony after flying in from Mumbai Tina had butterflies in her stomach as she walked into the auditorium of the five-star hotel. It was full and the crowds made her nervous.

A people from all branches of the company milled around. She quickly made her way to the table reserved for her and sat down.

Soon, the CEO arrived. She couldn't see his face as he was surrounded by people. She had been hoping all this while for a chance to meet him. He was quite the go-getter and she was glad he would be handing over the award to her.

Tina had leaned back on her chair, taken a sip of the champagne and was ready to enjoy the evening when the emcee introduced the CEO. As he walked up to the podium, Tina took a sharp breath. His face was very familiar. She racked her brains to figure out who he was. There was a big round of applause when her turn came and as she walked up to the stage, her eyes met Bhasin's eyes.

"Hey," he said. "Hi," Tina responded before accepting the award. "Recognise me?" he asked. Then she knew. "Aakash, for AK Bhasin, Jassi's brother?" she asked. "Yes, he replied, "Let's talk later."

As the evening wore on and the auditorium grew more crowded, Tina suddenly wanted to leave. Congratulations had poured in and she was now tired from all that smiling and shaking of hands. Aakash had been surrounded by senior employees so she did not dare walk up to him for a chat.

Back in her room by 10.30 pm, Tina organised

her travel bag for the flight back the next morning. She had just got into bed after a long call with her parents to share details of the event when the phone in her room rang. "There's a call for you," the operator said, "Connecting..."

The voice at the other end was deep and husky. "Hey Tina, hope you have not forgotten me."

"Akash, sorry, sir..." she said, fumbling with her words because she couldn't figure out how to address him. He laughed at that and soon Tina too joined in.

"Don't say, sir, Tina. I am not calling you as a boss. I was so surprised and pleased to see you today and really proud to see what you have achieved."

Tina could tell he was being genuine. "The feeling is mutual. I am so happy you are our CEO."

"Well, that's great then. Let's meet tomorrow for breakfast at 9.30 sharp," he said. "I'll see you down at the restaurant."

"That will be wonderful," said Tina. "Look forward to it."

Chapter-22
Acting on impulse

Next morning, very businesslike in her blazer and jacket, Tina walked to the restaurant for breakfast. Just as she was looking around trying to locate Aakash. A waiter walked up to her and escorted her to a specially reserved room virtually spilling over with flowers and lit candles. Aakash was waiting and rose from his chair to greet her when she entered. "I reserve this room for special meetings," he smiled, pulling her chair out.

Both of them talked while enjoying a sumptuous breakfast and did not know how an hour had passed by in a flash. Much reluctantly, Tina said, "I have to leave now, my flight to Mumbai leaves in a couple of hours."

"Don't worry, I will get it canceled if you want," Aakash laughed, as Tina looked at him, not understanding what he meant.

"I was just kidding. Don't take me seriously. But if you don't want to go let me know and I will arrange for another flight ticket," said

"Why should I not go?" Tina retorted. "Today is Sunday. I have work tomorrow. And what will I do in Delhi?"

"Well, we've met only twice and have had such a good time. I believe we should meet more often, don't you think so?" He said with a twinkle in his eyes.

Tina was confused as she was not prepared for this, but from what she had heard from Jassi and seen now she knew Aakash was a very decent person. He was also her boss. It was tempting to take up his invitation to stay on in Delhi for a day.

"Don't worry, I have a plan in mind for you which is very exciting," he said.

Exciting? Tina's antennas were up at the thought of doing some really interesting work and so she decided she could stay back.

"Okay, boss," so what's the plan?" she said, saluting him.

"Well first we go see a movie. I will get the tickets booked," he said. "Let's start from there."

That made Tina uncomfortable. She thrived on working hard. Going to the movies with a good looking man was definitely not on her agenda. His openness was also too much to handle.

As she wrung her hands, unable to decide, she reminded herself of the times when she had been on her own, waiting for friends to call but they had been too busy applying to colleges. Then there were those dark days at the hospital when she was struggling with depression. Have a fling with destiny. Take a leap of faith when you can, she advised herself.

"I take time to accept things, but one thing I know. I am very happy that I met you again. We had such a good time when we met last time and gorged on all the food in the university canteen. It's such a coincidence that I bumped into you. So yes, I shall stay for a day," she told him.

"Okay then," he said, beaming. "Hooray for today."

"Yes, let's just let our hair down," she said.

They planned to go shopping first and then see a movie. "See you in the lobby," Aakash said.

I'll just freshen up and get back," she replied excitedly.

"No, not so fast. Call me when you are ready. I will wait for you outside in the car," he said.

Tina realized that he was not ready to meet her in public with all the prying eyes and gossips around. She liked him for that.

Chapter-23
An irresistible offer

Tina called Aakash when she was ready and took the elevator to the lobby. He had texted her his car number so it did not take her long to find it. Aakash was at the wheel. He had changed into jeans and a white T-shirt and looked really young.

As Tina reached, she stared at him for a few seconds. "What's wrong," he asked. "Is something wrong with my face?"

"No," she giggled. "You remind me of the same young Aakash I had met three years ago. And now you are CEO."

"I am still the same, Tina, I haven't changed," he replied. Discussing the news and arguing over politics, both reached the shopping mall in no time at all.

Tina felt happy and relaxed after a very long time. Both wandered around, looking at the show windows. And as he stretched out his hand to hold hers, Tina gave in. It's lighthearted fun, she told herself, so might as well enjoy it.

It was quite a shopping spree. Tina bought some beautiful outfits, rolling with laughter when Aakash gave her his very funny take on what worked for her and what did not as she modeled them for him after coming out of the trial room.

She said a short prayer to God too, for her fantastic job with a great salary that allowed her to live such luxurious lifestyle.

Aakash too got himself a couple of T-shirts before she located one of her favourite restaurants from her university days and insisted she treat him for lunch.

He smiled to see her so excited, looking around in wonder, commenting on the changes in décor and new additions to the menu. "You look so thrilled," he said.

"Yes, I missed this place so much," she grinned. "Then why don't you come here and work," he said.

"Well, I love my work. Why should I leave it and what if I don't get a job here?" She asked.

"We could always do with a solid hand at work in Delhi. I could get you a transfer here," Aakash suggested.

"Really?" Tina's eyes widened. "Could you manage that?"

"Well, the CEO can do anything," said Aakash, airily. "On a serious note though. We can get you permanently on to that project and I am sure you will really enjoy it."

Tina was really happy. That meant she would be closer to Dehradun, ready to drop everything and be with her parents if they needed her. Many of her friends from university days were also here, which would mean a better social life. "Less commuting compared to Mumbai," Tina quipped. "I will take up your offer."

"If you are serious I can talk to management," he said.

"Thank you," she hugged him spontaneously before realising what she had done and sank back in her chair red with embarrassment.

"You are most welcome," he said affectionately.

After some sightseeing and then watching a movie both returned to the hotel room. Aakash walked with her to her room and left after bidding her a quick goodnight.

Watching him go, Tina felt good about him and his values.

But most of all, the thought of moving to Delhi brought a smile to her face.

Chapter-24
The surprise proposal

Tina received her joining letter signed by Aakash from the Delhi office. She immediately called her parents to give them the good news.

"Now we have to find you a Delhi boy," Sarika said. "Just say the word and we will start looking."

"No thanks, mummy. I will let you know when I am ready," Tina said.

The next few days were chaotic with Tina winding up her household and tying up all the loose ends at work. Most of her luggage and sundry goods were packed and carted away. Farewell parties were planned too by many people at the office who were sad to see her go.

There were more responsibilities to handle at the Delhi office so Tina got busy with work immediately, not getting time to really enjoy the beautiful two-bedroom flat she was given with the job.

She was determined to deliver results at work as Aakash had reposed a lot of faith in her and she did not want to let him down.

Soon, she had settled in. Often she bumped into Aakash and stopped to share information about work or some coffee with him. They dated on and off on weekends, and slowly, though it was nothing serious, a bond was beginning to develop between them.

Aakash, a thorough gentleman, was very careful to ensure that their interactions at work remained strictly professional with no complaints about their conduct.

What Tina also liked about Aakash was his respect for her and her ideas. Never once did he step out of line when it came to his behaviour, both outside and in office.

As work kept her busy, Tina lost count of time, realising quite late that two years had passed on the job and she was approaching a milestone. It would be her 25th birthday in a couple of weeks and Tina, now corporate HR manager in her department, was planning to throw a party at a five-star hotel.

Her parents had come to town for the very special occasion and were staying with her. People dressed up to the nines and sang, danced and enjoyed themselves. They were all fond of Tina and cheered loudly when she blew out all the candles in one go and then cut the cake.

Suddenly Aakash sprang a surprise by picking up the mike. As Tina looked on, he said, "I met Tina five years ago and have got to know her well over the last two years. She is as simple as she used to be at university. Yes, even I didn't know she had joined our company but remembered our first meeting when I handed her an award. She has not changed from the simple girl she used to be years ago even though she is one of our star performers, much loved by her colleagues and bosses."

As people gathered around him, he continued, "Today, on her birthday, I wanted to give her something special. Tina, please come here."

As she walked up to him, Tina felt the blood rush to her face. He had pulled out a box from his pocket and opened it to reveal the most beautiful ring she had seen.

A loud cheer went up. Sarika and Jayant watched in amazement but Tina went numb, looking into Aakash's eyes with a bewildered expression. Bending on one knee, he held up the ring and said, "Will you marry me, Tina?"

As she looked around, not knowing what to do, her friends started shouting, "Say yes Tina. He is the man for you."

Sarika was crying. She had met and grown very fond of Aakash during her trips to Delhi and hoped secretly for his union with her daughter to come about.

Still not ready to commit, Tina felt her options were limited. Yes, she loved Aakash in her own way, but was it enough? She knew if she said no, many hearts in that room, including that of the people she loved most, her father, mother and Aakash, would break.

It was hard to believe that this big shot, a man so many people looked up to, wanted to share his life with her, Tina,who was rejected so cruelly years ago by the boys and girl she had loved.

Aakash had chosen to declare his love for her not in private but at a party before all of his employees. He wanted them to be with him on this most special day and share his happiness. It showed how genuine he was and how much he valued her and his people.

"Yes," she said, "I will."

As the room erupted in cheers his arms enfolded her in a hug. "Yes, I know you love me too," he said.

Tina smiled.

Even as they were surrounded by people, including a dazed Sarika and Jayant, congratulating and hugging them, she turned her head to look out of the windows of the auditorium high above Delhi's traffic to fill the vacuum in her heart.

Chapter-25
Conditional love

Life changed drastically for Tina. Aakash, her best friend, was now her fiancée. She was treated with much courtesy at work.

Tina also understood that their relationship would now demand more intimacy, especially when it came to Aakash.

Though he had never crossed limits and they had often hugged and cuddled when left alone, he respected Tina's boundaries and understood that past hurts had left deep scars in her psyche.

Tina's own sense of guilt was killing her now. She knew she could not go forward without telling him about her sexuality. Yes, it had been years since she had been attracted to a woman, but she knew what happened with Shruti and Alisha were very real experiences, something which she could not deny to herself or hide from the man she loved.

But then, warned another little voice in her head, she should also not allow her past to jeopardise her beautiful present. She was madly in love with this man and wanted him to be a part of her life at any cost. Keeping a secret from him was the only thing gnawing away at her conscience.

"I should dedicate a hundred percent of my life to Aakash and keep him happy," she thought to herself.

By and by she realized that no matter how much she reasoned with herself, she had to chalk out a middle path for both of them for their own survival. So she called him home for dinner on a Sunday, something that made Aakash very happy as she had taken the initiative for the very first time plan something for them together.

Reaching her apartment before time, he was, however, a little shocked to see Tina open the door with a cigarette in her hand and the living room full of smoke. A non-smoker himself, he had not known about this habit of hers, nor had she told him about it.

As they sat down Tina continued to smoke. She looked troubled, not her usual giggling, happy self. After some time, as both sat in silence with Aakash waiting for her to talk, she stubbed the cigarette butt in the ashtray and asked, "are you not surprised to see this? I know I should have told you earlier but I don't smoke every day. But today I want to."

Smiling, he held her hand and looked into her eyes. "What's the matter. Are you not happy with our engagement? I know I announced it without asking you, but I wanted to give you a surprise. I know you love me."

"I love you more than myself," Tina replied, "and I am happy for both of us, but…"

"But what Tina?" asked Aakash, now worried.

"I am still not ready for a commitment," was her response.

"We are committed already. You said yes at your birthday party, remember?" He said.

Tina didn't answer. She got up from her chair to sit close to him. Looking straight into his eyes she said, "Yes, we are committed, but living together in a committed relationship under one roof is a different thing entirely."

"I do understand what you are trying to say, but what's the problem in getting married? We love each other, so getting legally married and planning one life together is how it should be done," he said.

When she heard him, Tina sighed, frustrated, and got up to go, but Aakash held her hand to pull her down on her chair again.

"Don't run, Tina. Tell me what you want."

"I want a live-in relationship first and then think about getting married," she replied, much to Aakash's surprise. He had always thought of her as someone who dreamt of getting married and having children.

This was something else entirely.

"Are you sure about what you are saying? Have you thought about your family and my family too? What are they going to say? Would they agree?"

He was surprised to see this stubborn streak in her. "It is about us, right?" Tina asked. "We have to live together. It is about our future."

"Can't we have our future after marriage?" Aakash interrupted her.

"We can," Tina replied but I want us to spend some time together without labelling our relationship. Don't you trust our relationship?"

Aakash understood that Tina had already made up her mind and nothing was going to change it now.

He said, "Okay, I am fine with it, but we have to move to Mumbai because people there are more tolerant of such arrangements."

"Yes, anywhere," Tina was rude this time, upsetting Aakash. But he was sure that there was a valid reason behind her decision.

And he was determined to find out what it was. He loved her.

Chapter-26

Reawakening

Tina's parents took a long time to accept her decision to live-in with Aakash. After heated discussions both finally relented to the couple's decision to move to Mumbai, far away from their relatives and friends.

Though he took time to shift the CEO's zone of operations to another city Aakash ensured it was done quickly and efficiently.

As both began their life in a beautiful sea-facing flat in Juhu, Tina finally accepted how good they were for each other. She took on her duties very seriously and was a wonderful, caring partner to Aakash.

Romantic movies, dinners, dates, hanging around in beaches, they did it all.

Though both worked hard to ensure that the move did not have any impact on the company or Tina's department, their personal life, they felt, was a beautiful journey.

Their growing intimacy too was wonderful. Tina found it all very delightful and wondered why she had hesitated initially to allow Aakash into her life as her lover. He was sensual, skillful and knew how to press all of her right buttons in the bedroom.

Slowly, both were learning and growing with each other, accepting their wants and needs and making sure that the other person did not feel unloved or unwanted in any way.

Both had a quiet birthday celebration when she turned 26. Aakash surprised her by decking up the apartment with her favourite lilies and scented candles. When she reached home by 7pm thinking he was away to another part of town meeting clients the apartment was in darkness. As she switched on the fan and lights she laughed out loud with delight when rose petals fluttered down on her from the fan.

"How pretty it looks," she exclaimed as Aakash came into the room, took her bag and shoes away from her and lifted her in his arms. He undressed her and took a shower together.

A beautiful new pristine white gown was laid out on the bed strewn with rose petals. When she wore it she looked ethereal, like a mermaid emerging from white clouds.

After the cake was cut and both enjoyed the fabulous Continental dinner he had ordered with sparkling white wine. Both of them spent an unforgettable night of passion which made her wonder how she had lived all those years without him.

Tina knew she had surrendered to this beautiful man with her mind, body, and soul, and nothing else could complete her as he did.

The next morning was all the more special as he brought tea for her in bed and woke her with a kiss on the forehead. "But let's not make a habit of it," he joked. "Birthdays are special so you are allowed to sleep in." Both of them giggled like little children.

Reading the newspaper together in bed, her head on his shoulder, Tina examined her heart and realized, she was at peace. No one could have given her what he had, and with so much love.

It was a weekend so Tina showered first and made breakfast while Aakash was in the washroom. When he walked over to the table a handwritten note was waiting for him. "What's this," he said, mystified. "Read it," Tina said, biting on her buttered toast, her eyes sparkling with mischief.

He exclaimed with joy when he opened it. "Let's

get married," Tina had written.

Elated, he lifted her up in his arms and danced around with her in the apartment, gleefully shouting "Yes, yes, yes."

Tina's parents were thrilled to hear the news. It was a simple ceremony with family and friends in attendance and lots of happiness and laughter.

Nothing changed except for the sense of security that Tina felt as a married woman. Each day was a revelation of how important it was to be responsible for a union that bound them together emotionally, spiritually and legally.

After four years together, during which both had worked as well as played hard, Tina and Aakash announced their pregnancy to loved ones. A baby would cement their relationship, she knew, marvelling at how she was looking forward to the patter of tiny feet in her life. Arranging a nursery, buying clothes and toys, keeping a bag ready for her nursing home stay, Tina managed it all with Aakash's help.

Their healthy, cuddly baby boy, when he arrived, was named Parth and took over their lives completely. Every moment of Tina's maternity leave was spent with the little one, answering his every demand and smothering him with motherly love.

She couldn't have had it any other way.

All the darkness of Tina's past vanished when she brought Parth into this world.

Happy times seem to go by more quickly than sad ones. From her rejoining work to getting a full-time amazing nanny, to Parth's first day at school, to his academic achievements, his birthdays and milestones, Tina and Aakash felt every moment in their life with their son was a celebration.

Both had achieved a lot at work and made sure at the same time that they made no compromises with Parth's upbringing, ensuring he had turned out to be a well-rounded individual who knew how to take care of others' interests as well as his own. years passed on.

It was Parth's 18th birthday. All of his friends and relatives had been invited for a party in the evening. Tina and Aakash planned every little detail from the party favours to the cake to the balloons, streamers and games. Still the romantic lovebirds, they coordinated their clothing and happily greeted and took care of their guests.

After he had cut the cake and enjoyed a wonderful dinner with his family and guests, Parth left home for a movie with his friends.

Both Tina and Aakash settled in for the night with a video. As he brought in coffee they were soon absorbed in the story of a woman who was sexually assaulted by a member of her own family.

She had however healed and had moved on from the terrible experience to make a name for herself in the business world. Something about it disturbed Tina. The woman's struggles, her trauma and pain touched the darkest part of her heart that had remained hidden all these years.

The credits were flashing on the screen when Tina finally became aware of her surroundings. She looked around to find Aakash asleep. Something seemed to have changed in her. She went to the bathroom, washed her face and got into bed again, holding her sleeping husband tightly.

She woke up with a start and looked at the clock. It was 2 am. Her heart was beating very fast and she seemed breathless. The world was quiet except for the sound of Aakash's breathing.

Getting out of the bed and looking at herself in the bathroom mirror, Tina saw someone she did not recognise. Her face was red, her hair disheveled, her eyes bloodshot.

Hot water cascaded over her as she stood under the shower in her nightgown, looking up. Why now? Why these memories? Why these dreams?

Quietly, Tina removed her clothing and dropped in on the floor, tiptoeing to her cupboard to get a fresh set of pyjamas and T-shirt. She then sat on a chair, staring at Aakash, feeling as if she had lost control over her mind… that someone else had taken over.

After some time she got up and walked to the store room and pulled out an old briefcase of hers, taking out a bunch of old photographs. She gazed at one in which she and Aakash were standing together, arms around each other, on holiday.

She tore it to pieces.

Crying, tormented, rocking on a chair that she had dragged into the store room, her head between her legs, she kept repeating "Why? Why now? Why do I get such dreams? I am not bisexual. I love Aakash."

For her most shocking revelation, it was Alisha again, in, her dream, both were entwined together, their bodies naked and glistening, as real as real could be.

Tina thought she was going mad. Not now, when she was the mother of a wonderful son and an adorable husband.

It was a horrible reawakening and she could not do anything about it.

Tina left the store room as it was, wrote a letter to Aakash, checked up on Parth who had returned home in the early hours. He was asleep too, lost to the world.

Destiny had left her with no choice. A cab was available. She got out of the house, shut the door with a final click and was walked to the car.

She looked back. The house got smaller and then disappeared altogether.

Chapter-27
Fleeing

The next morning Aakash and Parth looked everywhere for Tina but couldn't find her. It made no sense. The old briefcase was lying open in the store room, torn pieces of their photograph scattered all around. Tina's night-clothes were on the floor, soaking wet.

It was a nightmare for Aakash. Where had Tina disappeared? Why didn't she wake him up? What happened to her? Never once in her life since they had been together had she not informed him about her whereabouts.

His heart went cold as he spotted the note on the dining table. Gripped with a sense of foreboding he opened it, his eyes widening in shock as he went through its contents before throwing it away and sinking in the sofa, his head in his hands.

She had finally confessed to her inner turmoil. She was bisexual. Her feelings had started to haunt her. She could not lie, she wrote, to the man she loved. Her love for him had forced her to face the truth.

Revisiting past events again and again from their first meeting to the last, Aakash couldn't believe what he had just read. Tina was an open book. Never once had she given him an indication of what she claimed to be.

Enraged and frustrated, he started throwing things around, screaming out her name. "Tina, Tina, where are you? Why did you do this?"

Hearing this, Parth, who was calling his grandparents from the other room to inform them about Tina, came running in. "Calm down dad," he said, putting his arms around his raging father. "I promise you we will do everything to get mom home. Calm down and think."

Silently Aakash passed the letter to him. How long was he going to hide Tina's secrets from her son? Parth was grown up enough to understand. Then, Aakash reasoned, you don't hide secrets, no matter how dark, from the people you love.

Parth understood how hurt his father was and how cheated he felt. He loved his mother more than his life, but Tina's truth was as hard to digest as the reality that chosen to leave them and go away.

Parth knew his father needed him now, more than ever, so he had to suppress his grief and be the man of the house.

Quick decisions were required… that his father was too distraught to take, so Parth first took Aakash to his room and asked him to get ready should they need to go to the police or to handle friends, family or office colleagues enquiring about Tina's whereabouts.

He then tried calling Tina on her cellphone, but it had been switched off.

Both men got ready and sat down together at the dining table to take a call on the move forward. They had Tina's letter and knew that going to the police would only lead to more complications. Everyone would know and speculate over Tina's sexual orientation. Their marriage too would come under scrutiny. Had all those years of togetherness been wasted? As angry and bewildered as they were, Aakash and Parth knew they could not leave Tina vulnerable and exposed by this revelation. "We need to think. We need to find out where she is. Inform the office. Learn about what decision she wants to take. Tina's parents have to be informed," Akash was businesslike, back to being the man in charge.

He had taken the first step towards normalcy. It would take a long, long time to come to grips with the situation, but he and Parth were going to make it, he convinced himself.

The two most important men in Tina's life knew they had each other to rely on even though the woman they loved the most had let them down.

* * *

Tina checked into a hotel on the other part of town. She still did not understand what it was that made her walk away from her happy home, but knew that things were out of her control now.

Tired and broken, with Parth and Aakash constantly on her mind, she cried endlessly, unable to bear the thought of the grief she had caused them.

Would she ever see them again? Would they accept her for who she was? How could they live with a woman who had taken such a long time to come to terms with her own truth?

Sleeping fitfully and crying the whole day, she called her parents once to tell them that she had left home and that Aakash was in no way responsible for her decision.

She said she would keep calling them to let them know she was safe and that they should convey her messages to her son and husband too so that they don't worry.

Before Sarika and Jayant could say anything, she said "I will be able to look after myself, don't worry. Take care of them," she wept, ended the call and switched off her phone.

Crying the whole day and sleeping fitfully, Tina did not eat a morsel that day.

The next morning, feeling somewhat grounded, she showered, wore a fresh set of clothes she was carrying in a bag and went out to a restaurant nearby for a cup of tea and toast.

What would she do next? The thought turned into a knot in her heart, squeezing it until she was unable to breathe. Once back in her room, she picked up her phone and scrolled through the numbers.

Alisha's name popped up. One thing she had made sure through all these years was to ensure that her number had not been deleted from her phone book.

Would Alisha have changed the number? Would she remember her and acknowledge her existence? What would she say to her? Just thinking about things would not help, Tina decided. She called the number once, twice, a number of times, but no one picked up.

Tina also saw Parth's missed call but did not dare call him back.

She paced up and down in her room for hours

before finally collapsing on the bed and falling into a dreamless sleep.

Her eyes flew open suddenly some hours later. The phone flashed the time: 4 am. Not thinking, Tina called Alisha's number again. This time someone picked up. It was a sweet, soft voice. "Alisha?" She asked. "No," was the response, "Ma'am is busy carrying out her early morning rituals. Please call after 6am."

Tina could not fall asleep after that. Waiting impatiently, she dialed Alisha once again at 6.15 am. She picked up this time. "Hello," Tina said.

"What a pleasant surprise, Tina. I am so happy you called finally," Alisha spoke, her voice beautiful and soothing. Tina was surprised to hear this because she had always been under the impression that Alisha had left Dehradun upset because Tina had been unwilling to take their relationship forward.

"I am so glad to hear your lovely voice after a long time," Tina said. "I wanted to call but could not. I am very sorry for whatever happened between us." Everything she had wanted to say over the years tumbled out.

"I am sorry too for my immature behavior," Alisha responded. "How are you doing? I heard from my sister that you have a great career now and a lovely husband and a son. How is your family doing? You must be very happy. You deserve everything,

Tina."

Expecting to hear a wonderful account of Tina's life, Alisha was surprised to hear her sobbing.

"What happened? Why are you crying?" She asked.

When Tina shared her story Alisha said she could well imagine the pain she was going through. "Please don't cry. Listen, come over to Hyderabad. I am running an NGO here. Spend some time with us and you will feel better. Are you listening to me?" She asked. "I am texting you my address immediately."

Tina was relieved to know that Alisha intended to sort out her dilemma. "I know you love your family very much. But don't worry, give them some time. They also love you and will understand you," she assured the distraught woman.

The text message came instantly. Tina walked to a travel agent nearby and booked a flight ticket. For the first time in three days she was seeing some light.

"Come soon," Alisha urged her. She was concerned and knew it was not good for Tina to stay alone in a hotel when she had, had a mental breakdown.

By the next evening she was in Hyderabad and was delighted to see Alisha, now very serene, strands of grey in her hair. Both hugged each other and Alisha showed her to her room and asked her to rest first as she looked tired and gaunt.

"I will send you dinner and we will talk in the morning," she said.

Tina changed and climbed into bed. Sleep when it came was very sweet.

Chapter-28
Divine guidance

Tina woke up at 8am after hearing a knock on the door. She opened it to find Alisha's glowing smile greeting her. "How are you feeling?" She asked.

"Better," Tina replied.

"Then come down for breakfast, I am waiting outside in the garden," her host said.

"Catch you in 15 minutes after I freshen up," Tina responded.

When she stepped out into the green lawns shaded by tall trees she found Alisha giving a bunch of youngsters all sorts of gardening tips. When she introduced them to her Tina was surprised to learn that they were trans people and others from LGBTQ groups. Some of them were very young – just 12 to 18 years old, while others were middle-aged.

Her NGO helped LGBTQs, Alisha explained. The effort was to make them as well as society accept their sexual orientation.

It was a happy group. They worked hard in the garden and told Tina about their passions and their plans for life.

Alisha had to call her twice before Tina found the heart to leave the "happy people," as she called them, to join her in the cafeteria and have breakfast.

It was a beautiful place all done up in rainbow colours. Breakfast was served by smiling volunteers who seemed to like Tina.

Enjoying the crisp dosa and chutney, she questioned Alisha about the noble initiative which was helping out around 200 people. When she went on a tour of the place with Alisha she saw everyone smiling and cheerfully carrying out duties assigned to them.

From education to other skills such as cooking and craftwork, everything was taught to them under one roof. It was their own world, a cosy cocoon where there was no judgement, no trial, no tribulation and most importantly, no hatred.

"What led to this," she asked Alisha? "How did you get the idea to launch the NGO?"

"A failed relationship did it," was the response. Alisha's boyfriend in college had dumped her when he learnt about her bisexuality. It had taken her a long time to come to terms with his rejection, but she had started healing after she started working with the NGO.

"Last year, the owner of this place put me in charge and went abroad to manage other projects there," she said.

The NGO was taking care of LGBTQ people abandoned by their families and teaching them self-love and acceptance before equipping them with skills to be mainstreamed.

Tina was happy, convinced that she had received divine guidance to fulfill her life's purpose. "I want to help and contribute to this noble cause," she said.

"I know," Alisha smiled. "Get working," she ordered her before walking away.

Chapter-29
Reaching out

Tina was up bright and early the next morning, raring to go. Reporting to Alisha after bath and breakfast, she was given a couple of cases to handle. Most of the people she had to connect with were from upper class backgrounds, but they needed to figure out their sexual orientation and chalk out a path for themselves in society and live fulfilled lives. They were English-speaking and needed to communicate with someone who would understand them.

An intelligent person like Tina with an HR background, someone who had suffered in life trying to find her own identity, was the ideal person to handle them, Alisha reasoned.

One of the persons Tina was assigned to was a 35-year-old woman who had been disowned by her family after she came out as a lesbian.

When Tina knocked at her door, the pretty woman looked out quizzically, asking: "Can I help you?"

After she introduced herself Tina was invited in and a chair pulled out for her. The woman had been working on her computer. As Tina started asking her about her hobbies, interests and goals, she responded somewhat brusquely: "I can handle myself. I know you are a counsellor but you can't understand what it means to be a lesbian."

Very gently Tina said: "Well, I know what it means to be bisexual."

Immediately the other woman's expression softened. "I am sorry," she said.

"Why sorry? Your reaction was natural. Anyone would be offended if another person snooped in their lives," laughed Tina.

Surprised, the other girl started laughing too and both warmed up to each other. "We have to make everyone smile," Tina told her, holding her hand, adding "Are we a team now?"

The woman nodded and the two talked for some time, sharing their stories, discussing how others had come to terms with their identities and moved on in life to live gracefully, fearlessly and on good terms with themselves.

Before Tina knew it four months had passed.

She had started calling home too once in two weeks to speak to Aakash and Parth. Their anger had been hard to bear but each time their conversations lasted a little longer than before as they put their own emotions aside to try and understand what she was going through.

Her own pain was forgotten in her desire to reach out to the suffering. She had won numerous friends and admirers for her work. They said she added value to their lives through her soft skills, communications and her intelligence.

Often, she met and worked with parents of young LGBTQ people, probing their mindsets and fears and making them understand people's sexual orientation and how their life ceased to have meaning if their feelings were not acknowledged. Many parents were encouraged to reconcile with their children and take them home, defending their choices and preferences when others pointed fingers at them.

One afternoon when Tina had just started counselling a parent about her transgender son, Alisha called to say that she had visitors. Wondering who it could be Tina finished work and made her way to the office.,

Colour drained from her face when she opened the door and found Aakash and Parth, the husband

and son she had fled from, sitting at Alisha's desk with her. As her friend stepped out quietly to give them some privacy, Tina remained frozen, tears flowing from her eyes, a picture of guilt.

"I abandoned you. I did not know what to do," was all that she could manage.

There was no need for words. Parth ran to her and hugged her and it broke her heart to see him in tears. "Sorry, sorry, sorry," she said as she clung to him desperately, all the affection she had suppressed through these months overflowing from her heart.

"Please forgive me," she heard. Opening her eyes and looking beyond Parth's shoulder, she saw Aakash, his face haggard and tired, standing in front of them.

"Why should I forgive you when you should be the one doing all the forgiving," she wept, attempting to hug both men together. "I made the mistake of not telling you about myself and then running away like a coward when the truth came back to haunt me. I was a mess, I'm sorry," she said, burying her face in his chest. "I have always loved you and have never cheated on you. I understand that it was not my fault that I was born bisexual. I should have never hid it from you. Whether you accepted it or not would have been your choice."

"I should have been more understanding," Aakash replied, holding her close. "I should have listened to you instead of rushing you into marriage, tried to understand your dilemma. I have been introspecting and realise that two people make a marriage. It's a lot of work. But if you love someone you have to take whatever they bring with themselves, even if it is a truth you are not comfortable hearing," added.

"Your absence has forced Parth and me to realise that we can't live without you – without being in your life. We want to let you fly, do what you want."

"Please take us back," he pleaded. "Stay here, do the good work you are doing, but please get back to being a part of our lives. I want nothing else."

"I have accepted myself gracefully, Aakash, and I am teaching young people here to do the same. I would like to make this place my home and would love it if you join me here or let me visit you when I can," Tina replied.

"I love you both," she continued. "I know you need me and I need you, but these people need me more. I have my work cut out for me. I will be home when I can, to be with you… but duty compels me to stay here."

Parth hugged her tight. "I'll wait for you mum, and come to see you when I can."

"We will talk, sort out our lives. I will be happy if you are happy. I just needed to see that you are okay and want you to know that you have a home in Mumbai or any other place where we choose to settle," Aakash promised.

Holding her close and kissing her, he said, "Farewell for now, my love, both of us belong to you, always and forever."

And then they were gone, two hazy figures seen through a veil of tears even though Tina's heart was full of joy after reuniting with her loved ones again.

Chapter - 30

To stand alone in the crowd

Tina was quiet now. She was looking at me. I was speechless and found it hard to believe how courageous this woman was in giving up everything she had loved for a chance to help the wronged and the suffering.

Not knowing what to say or how to say it I got up from my chair and gave her a big hug. "I feel blessed that I met you and learnt about your struggles, victories and your amazing contribution to society. Thank you so much, Tina, for sharing your story with me."

"The pleasure is all mine," she replied. "Destiny chooses us for a purpose and I am glad I found my calling. Now it is your turn."

Both of us strolled in the garden, enjoying the

greenery and the cool breeze. Soon, laughing and chattering, a number of young people came out to us, bidding fond farewells to me and giving me beautiful gifts that they had made themselves.

Overwhelmed, I went back to my room to pack, carefully placing the diary with my notes on Tina's story in the flap of my suitcase.

Yes, it was my turn to tell her story to the world.

I switched off the lights and went off to sleep. I had to catch the early morning flight back to Chandigarh.

***

Epilogue

I feel a mix of emotions as I look back at the journey that led to this book. Gender and sexuality are subjects that are not given the importance they deserve. Anything beyond prescribed norms raises people's hackles and arouses strong emotions. This gives birth to twisted notions and incorrect presumptions about people with a different sexual orientation.

As I say elsewhere in the book, prejudice keeps people away from accepting differences. Nowhere is this more true than in the case of sexuality.

My book aims to be a trailblazer, where the global society of today accepts differences just as easily as we accept technology.

Having said this, the book itself got tremendous support from friends and family and important members of society, including government officials.

Finally, all good things come to an end; the end of this book and its wide distribution, however, will only kick start a phase of my life that I will remember for a lifetime.

On this note, please take care. And if we can, be more compassionate and loving towards the people who may be different from us. They can't help who they are and have the right to live as peacefully as we do.